Sex Role Stereotyping In The Schools

Elizabeth Hirzler Weiner, Editor

National Education Association
Washington, D.C.

Library of Congress Cataloging in Publication Data
Main entry under title:

Sex role stereotyping in the schools.

(Aspects of learning)
Bibliography: p.
1. Sex differences in education—Addresses, essays, lectures. 2. Sex role—Addresses, essays, lectures. I. Weiner, Elizabeth Hirzler. II. Series: National Education Association of the United States. NEA aspects of learning.
LB1117.S42 1980   370.19'345   79-28102
ISBN 0-8106-1490-1

0057969

Acknowledgments

NEA gratefully acknowledges the permissions given to use the following: •"Images of Males and Females in Elementary School Textbooks in Five Subject Areas" by Lenore J. Weitzman and Diane Rizzo. Reprinted from *Biased Textbooks*. Copyright © 1974 by The National Foundation for the Improvement of Education. •"Sexual Stereotyping and Mathematics Learning" by Elizabeth Fennema and Julia A. Sherman. Reprinted from *The Arithmetic Teacher*, May 1977 (Vol. 24, pp. 369-372), Copyright © 1977 by the National Council of Teachers of Mathematics. •"Why Don't Girls Misbehave More Than Boys in School?" by Daniel Linden Duke. Reprinted from *Journal of Youth and Adolescence*, No. 2, 1978. •"Cutting Sex Bias Out of Voc Ed" by Phyllis Lehmann. *Worklife*, February 1977. •"Enlarging the American Dream" by Donna Hart. *American Education*, May 1977. •"Title IX Action Plan" as approved by the Board of Education, Montgomery County (Maryland) Public Schools, on June 27, 1977. •"Guide for Evaluating Sex Stereotyping in Reading Materials," prepared by the Committee on Sexism and Reading of IRA. *The Reading Teacher*, December 1977. •"The Why of a Workshop" by Mary Ellen Verheyden-Hilliard. Reprinted from *A Handbook for Workshops on Sex Equality in Education*, Sex Equity in Guidance Opportunities Project, the American Personnel & Guidance Association. •"Consciousness Razors" by Verne Moberg. National Education Association. •"Early Socialization" by Barbara Gates, Susan Klaw, and Adria Steinberg. Reprinted from *Changing Learning, Changing Lives*. Copyright © 1979 The Group School. Old Westbury, N.Y.: The Feminist Press. •"Consciousness-Raising Activities for Sixth-Grade Students" by Marilyn Roessler. Reprinted from *Strategies for Equality: Vol. 1, Guidance, Social Studies, Physical Education*. Training Institute for Sex Desegregation of the Public Schools, Rutgers, The State University of New Jersey, January 1978.

Editor

Elizabeth Hirzler Weiner was formerly a teacher in the Greenwich, Connecticut public schools; she is currently an educational researcher and writer. Ms. Weiner is the editor of two other NEA publications: *Unfinished Stories for Facilitating Decision Making in the Elementary Classroom* and *Discipline in the Classroom* (Second Revised Edition).

376.3
NAT

113494

Contents

Introduction

Seven years after passage of Title IX, the federal statute outlawing sex bias in the schools, the educational system still significantly narrows the life choices of millions of girls and women.

This was the charge of a study made by the Project on Equal Education Rights (PEER) of the National Organization for Women's Legal Defense and Education Fund as school opened in the fall of 1979.

After examining national progress in three key areas felt to be "traditional bellweathers of education sex bias," PEER charted the failures:

- Although women account for nearly seven out of 10 classroom teachers, they hold only one out of 10 top school administrative jobs.
- Only 11 percent of students in the traditionally male vocational programs of agriculture, technology, trades, and industry are girls.

True, there have been gains since 1972, with athletics taking the greatest leap from 18 percent female participation to 33 percent, and training programs for the higher-paying traditionally male jobs showing girls' enrollment up from 5 to 11 percent. But the meager 1 percent rise of women in the top school administrative posts dismally reaffirms the deeply entrenched presence of sex role stereotyping in our schools today.

While not the only contributing factor, much of the reinforcement of these traditional roles is caused by the attitudes and actions of school personnel, however inadvertent and unintended they may be. It comes through careless use of language and curriculum materials, through unrecognized differential treatment of students, and through an unwitting continuation of teachers' education and the role expectations held out to them throughout their own education.

"Most teachers are not guilty culprits," David Sadker, Director of the Mid-Atlantic Center for Sex Equity, was quick to say in an interview. "They simply are unaware that their daily actions promote sex bias and sex role stereotyping."

This volume, then, is designed first, to increase teacher awareness of how sex role stereotyping enters into and narrows the educational process and outcomes; secondly, to provide understanding of Title IX and its grievance procedures, and, finally, to offer teaching strategies for change.

The opening selection, "Forms of Sex Bias and Their Manifestations in the Classroom," acts as an introduction to *Part One: Sex Role Stereotyping in the School*. Excerpted from one of the excellent workshop kits now available, it cites the research that puts the lie to the commonly held "I-treat-all-my-students-the-same" myth, goes on to identify various forms of sex bias in the classroom, and urges teachers to face reality: "If teachers are to eliminate the sex bias that is reflected in instructional procedure. . .they must become aware that it exists."

With this goal in mind, other selections focus on specific areas—language, textbooks, mathematics—detailing the existence of sex bias, analyzing its modes of operation, and discussing its effects on students, whether "exclusionary," as in the use of traditional generic language (Johnson), "crippling," as are the latent messages found in textbooks (Weitzman and Rizzo), or simply the "fulfillment of the stereotyped expectation," for example, in mathematics "of a female head that's not much for figures" (Fennema and Sherman).

Consider misbehavior to realize how pervasive sex role stereotyping is. Duke hypothesizes that teachers' differential treatment may cause boys to misbehave more than girls, and raises the ironic likelihood that female misbehavior may increase right along with sex equity.

Teachers need to be aware of the implications of the important and controversial studies of math performance (Fennema and Sherman); that girls' turning away from mathematics has major lifelong implications—narrowed career choices, limited earning potential—in the same way that the subtle counseling of girls away from traditionally male dominated vocational classes keeps them relegated to "women's work," or those jobs at the lowest end of the pay scale (Lehmann).

Nor is counseling something that should be confined to the senior year and a special school office. Verheyden-Hilliard's argument is that given the reality of women's lives today:
- They make up almost 50 pecent of the labor force
- The divorce rate is up 127 percent since 1960, and rising
- Only one out of 10 women in divorced families receives child support from the fathers
- They are two-thirds of all the old people who are poor

Counseling for financial independence should begin in kindergarten and continue with a lot of "on-going talk and discussion."

Finally, since equity is for *all* girls as well as boys, two dimensions of sex role stereotyping that must be examined in a volume of this kind are the double jeopardy faced by minority women (Hart) and the rigid conformity to norms expected of boys (Sadker).

Part Two: The Law is included to give teachers a working knowledge of Title IX and its grievance procedures, providing a solid basis not only for compliance with its regulations but for taking positive action to eliminate the root causes of sex bias.

There are many ways a teacher can contribute to this process; in broadest categories, through improving the system (and its parts), through increasing self-awareness, and through increasing student awareness.

Specific plans directed to each of these areas are found in *Part Three: Teaching Strategies*. Today, after years devoted to needed consciousness raising, the leading edge of the push for eliminating sex role stereotyping is found in this action area. Excellent materials are available for conducting workshops with colleagues and/or community members, as are pertinent lesson plans and teaching units to use with students at all levels.

The range here is from a checklist to evaluate reading materials to a schoolwide Title IX Action Plan, from a simple sentence completion for use as a follow-up to a class discussion based on Sadker's "Being a Man," to "Early Socialization," a unit that explores how male and female roles are established in childhood.

These kinds of teaching units are particularly important if teachers are to vigorously undo the self-limiting stereotypes with which young people tie themselves to traditional sex roles and free students' minds to explore all their possible options.

The demographics of the family today make it an economic necessity for girls to realize their full earning capacity; a goal that only can be reached after sex role stereotypes cease to stand in the way of sex equity in education and training programs.

As for personal life, it has always been the stated goal of teachers to educate the individual to his or her fullest potential; it is time to act affirmatively on this issue, to eliminate thinking of his or her potential and deal only in human potential.

Elizabeth Hirzler Weiner

Forms of Sex Bias and Their Manifestations In the Classroom

(From *Implementing Title IX and Attaining Sex Equity: A Workshop Package for Elementary-Secondary Educators,* U.S. Department of Health, Education, and Welfare, Office of Education, 1978, Shirley McCune and Martha Matthews.)

If most of us are asked to think about the ways that students are treated differently in classes, we are inclined to say, "I treat all students just alike." Research has shown that there is a strong possibility that this is not the case. Each of us has grown up in a society where we have learned to expect different things of girls and boys and to respond to the behavior of girls and boys in different ways.

The most comprehensive [of this] research which indicates that the outcomes of the education programs provided for females and males are not equal [is that] of the National Assessment of Education Progress.[1] The Assessment found major disparities in educational achievement of males and females. Males outperformed females in four areas: mathematics, science, social studies, and citizenship.

In the other four areas measured, females consistently outperformed males to any large degree in only one (writing); maintained a slight advantage in one (music); and in the remaining two subjects (reading and literature) are above male achievement levels at age nine, then dropped to lag behind males by the young adult ages 26-35.

The puzzling result of the National Assessment is that in the male dominated areas (mathematics, science, social studies, and citizenship), males and females at age nine show scholastic achievement that is fairly equal. By age 13, however, females have begun a decline in achievement that continues downward through age 17 and into adulthood.

These results would suggest that the differences may not be the result of basic ability differences, but rather the impact of the socialization experience on students. The socialization of boys and girls includes the total number of experiences they have in the home and in the community. Most of these experiences we have little or no control over. As educators, however, it is our responsibility to identify those forms of differential treatment in the classroom that may contribute to the different outcomes for females and males. One of the ways that we can measure ultimate equality for students is that we would not find large differences in outcomes or

9

achievements of students on the basis of sex.

At this time let's begin to examine the classroom and the instructional activities provided in the classroom and see if we can begin to identify some of the factors that may lead to the differential outcomes which we've discussed. Before we explore the data regarding instructional procedures and teacher behavior and student outcomes, it is important that we understand the limitations of the research on the impact of teacher behaviors on student outcomes. First, much of the research on the effect of various types of classroom instruction has been done with white middle class students; it is not generalizable to the instructional treatment of minority students.

Second, some of the studies of teacher behavior and student performance provide conflicting results. This may be a normal reflection of the difficulty of trying to determine the effect of classroom experiences in long term outcomes when every student is exposed to a multitude of other experiences and variables.

Last, we have only recently recognized the need for research which focuses directly on differential treatment on the basis of sex, so our knowledge base is limited.

Despite the limitations of our knowledge as to the specific impact of various forms of differential treatment of students on the basis of sex, there is an overwhelming amount of evidence as to a pattern of sex differentiated treatment which results in different outcomes for females and males. It is our responsibility as teachers to identify as many of the various forms of differential treatment as possible and work to eliminate such differences.

There are many ways of classifying the various forms of differential treatment of females and males in the classroom. One way to think about the forms of bias is to identify six types of bias—exclusion, stereotyping, fragmentation, linguistic bias, imbalance, and unreality—as they are evident in the management of the classroom and instructional procedures. Let's examine each of these.

Invisibility

If we were to ask most teachers to recall their most memorable and/or outstanding students, it is likely that most of the names identified would be those of male students. In fact, there is a good deal of data to suggest that males are the salient and visible members of classrooms.

One way this saliency of males is identified in the classroom is through an analysis of the teacher's interaction patterns with students. Studies indicate that teachers have more interactions of all kinds with boys than with girls in the classroom. Boys are not only reprimanded more (one study shows them receiving eight to 10 times as many control messages as do girls), but they also appear to be talked to and listened to more frequently than their female counterparts.[2] In short, while the research is not conclusive it appears that a pattern is formed through which boys receive more of the teacher's active verbal attention.

10

More recent research is disclosing many subtle differences in the types of interaction which takes place between teachers and students. For example, one group of researchers has found that teachers most frequently reprimand boys for creating disturbance or discipline problems in the classroom. They most frequently praise boys for their academic performance. The praise and reprimand patterns for girls is nearly completely reversed. Teachers usually praise girls for non-academic behaviors—for being neat, clean, polite, and quiet. When girls receive negative or punitive messages it is usually for their academic performance.[3] Other studies indicate that boys tend to overestimate their academic skills whereas girls tend to underestimate their skills.[4]

Lisa Serbin and her colleagues have demonstrated other subtleties in the ways teachers differentially distribute praise to females and males in the classroom. She found that girls are more likely to receive positive reinforcement if they stand close to their teachers while the reinforcement for boys was not dependent on proximity to the teacher.[5]

In general the teacher interaction studies suggest that girls are less visible and less audible in classrooms than are boys. They seem to get less of the teacher's attention. Further, teachers are likely to offer them reward and praise not for academic performance but for being polite and quiet, and for proximity-seeking behavior.

Exclusion and invisibility may occur not only through interaction patterns, but also through the physical environment of the classroom. If posters, pictures, newspaper clippings, and other visual materials exclude females, students are being provided a six-hour-a-day lesson in bias through invisibility.

Stereotyping

"Oh no! The projector is broken again. I need a young man with some good mechanical aptitude who can come up here and fix it!"

"Girls, would you please pour the punch and pass out the refreshments for the party."

"Well, John, your performance in my class shows that you have good scientific aptitude. And I know from talking with you that you like working with people and helping them. Have you been thinking about medicine as a career—perhaps becoming a doctor?"

"Well, Joan, your performance in my class shows that you have good scientific aptitude. And I know from talking with you that you like working with people and helping them. Have you been thinking about medicine as a career—perhaps becoming a nurse or lab technician?"

Perhaps these comments—or different versions of them—may sound familiar to you. They are verbal reflections of the way teachers frequently stereotype students, assuming that the male half of our population has in common one set of abilities, interests, values, and roles and the female half of our population has in common another set of abilities, interests, values, and roles. Such stereotyping generally reflects oversimplified attitudes and completely ignores individual differences.

The stereotyping in the examples is explicit. However, when teachers hold biased expectations about student behavior, these may be transmitted more subtly. The term "teacher expectations" or self-fulfilling prophecy may elicit a variety of reactions among you because there have been so many conflicting reports about this phenomenon. You'll remember that several years ago Rosenthal and Jacobson[6] randomly designated an average of five children per class as academic "spurters."

The teachers were carefully given the names of the "spurters;" the findings of the study indicated that if teachers expected intellectual blooming in specific children, such gains would, in fact, result. Further, teachers described the randomly selected experimental children as being happier, more curious, more interesting, and having a better chance for success in later life than control subjects.

Since this pioneering study to uncover some of the teacher/pupil interactive dynamics, there have been numerous studies which attempt to replicate it with many conflicting conclusions. However, after a thorough summary of the research on teacher expectations, Braun indicates that philosophically and psychologically the phenomenon of teacher expectations must be considered seriously.[7]

There is only limited data on the differential expectations teachers hold for their female and male students. In one study junior high school teachers were asked to select adjectives that they felt would describe good male and good female students.[8] Here are their responses:

Adjectives Describing Good Female Students		Adjectives Describing Good Male Students	
appreciative	sensitive	active	energetic
calm	dependable	adventurous	enterprising
conscientious	efficient	aggressive	frank
considerate	mature	assertive	independent
cooperative	obliging	curious	inventive
mannerly	thorough		
poised			

These columns reflect stereotypes in miniature of the female and male roles.

In another study, Palardy investigated the effect of teacher's beliefs on pupils' achievement and concluded that if teachers believe that first grade boys will do as well in reading as girls, then this, in fact, will happen.[9] Conversely, if teachers do not expect boys to do as well as girls, then, in fact, their reading performance will be lower.

Braun concludes, as a result of his analysis of teacher expectations research: "Teachers need to be sensitized to the biases and stereotypes they hold and encouraged to examine these seriously in relation to their classroom behavior. After all, it is the 'teacher expectation of the pupil' and the vicious circle it triggers that will determine largely the child's self-image, and ultimately, academic success or failure."[10]

Stereotypes teachers hold for their students on the basis of sex, race, class, or ethnicity may be manifested not only in the interpersonal climate of the classroom but in the physical structure as well. Displayed materials, showing active boys and passive girls and showing women primarily or solely as homemakers and men engaged in a variety of occupations are continual visual reminders of limited options and alternatives.

Fragmentation/Isolation

Fragmentation or separation on the basis of sex is another way that bias emerges in instructional management of the classroom. There are many ways that this segregation occurs. Teachers may establish procedures which delineate separate lining-up procedures for female and male students. There may be various academic competitions set up with "the boys against the girls." There may be a single sex interest and work group established.

Sometimes single sex interest work and play groups emerge as a phenomenon of peer rather than teacher selection. Then bias may emerge not through teacher initiation but rather through teacher tolerance and acceptance. For example, in elementary school cases of the "all boys club-no girls allowed," teachers may shrug, smile and reflect on how the situation will change one day. However, these same teachers would in all likelihood find a situation of "no Jews, no Italians, no Blacks allowed" abhorrent and would intervene to stop racial, ethnic, or religious exclusion. Sex separation, whether actively initiated or passively tolerated by the teacher, encourages social and academic isolation of the sexes and denies equality of opportunity and experience.

As with the previous forms of bias, fragmentation and isolation may also appear in the physical arrangement of the classroom. If visual materials are separated so that there is a single bulletin board of famous contemporary women (or Blacks or Jews or Italians), the message is being transmitted that this group is somehow separated from and tangential to the cultural mainstream.

Linguistic Bias

The same forms of bias that characterize the language patterns in instructional materials may also be manifested in the teacher's verbal expression. If the teacher subsumes all people under the term mankind, refers to historical figures as our forefathers, continually uses the pronoun "he" to encompass both females and males, uses biased occupational terms, refers to adult males as "men" and adult females as "girls," uses or accepts student usage of slang terms that reduce women to animal status (chick, bitch, biddy, etc.), then a sex-biased perception of reality is created for students in that classroom.

Further, linguistic bias may be apparent in all forms of written communication in the classroom—visual displays, letters to students and parents, classroom tests, journals, newspapers, etc. The result is that both verbal and written communication complement each other to reinforce sexist perceptions.

Imbalance/Selectivity

Encouraging each student to reach his or her full potential is at the heart of the educational process. However, through imbalance in the nature of compensatory instruction and sex-biased selection of those in need of remediation, realization of goals is often denied.

Before we discuss imbalance of emphasis in the nature of compensatory instruction in our schools, it is important to take a brief look at what we know about sex differences in intellectual abilities and achievement patterns.

There are many considerations to keep in mind when discussing sex differences. For example, sex difference discussion focuses on *average* differences between males and females, and there is always a great deal of overlap between the sexes. Further, most of the research has been done on white middle class children and findings may not be generalizable to other groups. Studies which result in findings of sex differences are more likely to get published than are findings of no differences (null findings). Consequently, this may result in the establishment of a research data base that magnifies and exaggerates differences that may exist between the sexes. Finally, it is inaccurate to assume that an ability or behavior that is determined to be a sex difference is innate. There must be further study to discover whether the difference is innate or learned.

According to Jacklin, there appear to be two intellectual sex differences: verbal abilities and spatial visualization.[11] Starting at about the junior high school years, girls achieve higher average scores on tests of verbal ability while boys achieve higher average scores on tests of spatial visualization which measure the ability to mentally rotate objects on two and three dimensions. There is evidence that spatial abilities can be directly and quickly taught. There is also a good deal of discussion concerning the potential relationship of spatial visualization abilities to achievement in mathematics.

We find a pattern in which boys have more problems in areas of reading and verbal ability. Girls are more likely to be at a disadvantage in areas related to spatial abilities, mathematics, and science. It is now important to take a look at the selection and balance with which compensatory instruction is delivered in our schools.

For years educators have been pondering why Johnny can't read, and the educational literature is filled with articles analyzing the problem and positive solutions. Further, when we consider the nature of the compensatory instruction offered by our school systems, we become aware that a key emphasis in this special instruction is on reading and verbal skills—the main problem areas for boys. In fact, the population serviced by this special instruction is primarily male. According to Gillespie and Fink, one of the "more interesting stable phenomenon in special education [is] that many more boys than girls are in need of special services."[12]

There are many possible explanations proffered as to why males appear to be in greater need of special instruction. However, increasing numbers of educators have begun to consider that there may be more males receiving special instruction because we have selected and emphasized that area of intellectual disadvantage which is most troublesome to male students.

Only recently have educators begun to ponder why Anne can't do math and why Sally has such a weak comprehension of even basic scientific principles. Only recently have some educators begun to consider that spatial skills should be taught in our classrooms. And only recently have special programs emerged to help alleviate the particular problems that female students are more likely to have in the area of mathematics. This is particularly critical because so many female students avoid taking math courses and math has become the "critical filter" that denies females access to a wide array of occupations.

Unreality

When teachers are asked whether they use different instructional procedures for their female and male students, they often express shock and denial. "Of course not," is a typical response. "I treat girls and boys in my classroom just the same." However, when these same teachers are observed, differential instructional patterns are clearly observable.

If teachers are to eliminate the sex bias that is reflected in instructional procedures, it is critical that they recognize the *reality* of this bias. They must become aware that it exists.

Perhaps one of the reasons that it is difficult for us to recognize the reality of differential treatment in our classroom is that we may not have examined the reality of the changes in our lives. We know that one of the major changes in the lives of women has been their entry into the paid labor force. Nine out of ten female students in our classrooms today will find it necessary to work outside the home sometime in their lives. Yet we continue to present images to females and males that are not consistent with this reality. Until we help female and male students to understand the reality of what they can expect for their adult lives—that women and men will be sharing work in paid employment and at home—only then will we be meeting the needs of the students we teach.

When sex bias is reflected in the very nature of the instructional process, the potential outcome is the loss of self-affirmation and esteem, loss of academic and occupational potential, denial of equal opportunity and limitations set on our students' alternatives and options. Until teachers understand and act on the need to eliminate differences in the teaching of females and males, only then will we be able to implement Title IX fully and attain sex equity.

Sexism in Language: The Case for Including Everybody

By Carole Schulte Johnson

Why are men who are forgetful called absent-minded while forgetful women are called scatterbrain? Why are men who are interested in everything referred to as curious but women of the same type are called nosy? Most people agree, as the foregoing illustrates, that word choices are a subtle way of stereotyping. That aspect of language, although important, is not the sole way that language can evoke biased responses. This discussion is centered on one aspect of language which tends to engender bias, the traditional generic usage in the English language. The question must be asked: Is traditional generic usage in language simply one of preference, or are there implications, beyond mere preference, which ought to be taken seriously by educators?

The position presented here is that traditional generic usage constitutes exclusionary language: that is, it excludes females in effect, if not by intent, because words such as policeman and mailman, allegedly gender-generic, tend to be interpreted as being gender-specific. Terms such as saleswomen exclude males in effect as well as by intent. Inclusionary language, on the other hand, does not exclude, either by intent or effect, on the basis of sex.

Writers from various disciplines, for example, linguists (Key, 1972; Lakoff, 1972), social scientists (Bosmajian, 1972; Kidd, 1971), educators (Burr, Dunn, and Farquhar, 1972; Tiedt, 1973), and a theologian (Russell, 1976), have written on the subject of language bias and have included the generic use of pronouns and "man" in their analyses.

Several studies are of special interest because subjects were asked to react to different ways of using language. Kidd had college students respond to 18 statements in which the masculine pronoun and "man" were

16

used in traditional generic fashion. They identified each pronoun antecedent according to several characteristics, including sex. The first nine statements were open-ended so that the sex of the referent would be identified as either male or female or both.

The potentialities of *man* are infinitely varied and exciting.

Social Status _____   Financial Position _____
Sex _____   Race _____

The second nine statements were in a forced-choice format:

How can we help a child to know his feelings? We can do so by providing a mirror to *his* emotions.

a. female-male   c. white-black
b. successful-unsuccessful   d. rich-poor

Subjects did not respond inclusively to the generic pronoun "man" either in the free or forced-choice format. In the free-choice, males were selected 407 times and females 53 times. Kidd concluded that the generic pronoun "man" is not generally interpreted as representing a neutral antecedent; it is, in fact, considered male.

College students turned in newspaper and magazine pictures to illustrate a proposed sociology textbook for Schneider and Hacker (1973). Two forms of chapter titles were used. Both contained eight common titles such as Culture and Ecology, neutral in gender. In addition, one form used five "man"-associated labels such as Industrial Man and Economic Man, while another contained comparable inclusionary titles, Industrial Life and Economic Behavior. They found that 64 percent of students receiving "man" titles submitted pictures containing only males, compared with 50 percent of those receiving the inclusionary titles. The authors concluded that a significantly large number of students did not interpret "man" generically.

Bem and Bem (1973) asked high school seniors to rate 12 job advertisements on an interested-uninterested scale. Eight ads, identical on all three forms, contained inclusionary language. The language of four telephone ads varied; operator and service representative (considered traditionally female) and frameman and lineman (considered traditionally male). The company's usual exclusionary language was used in Form I. Form II employed inclusionary language while Form III used sex-reversed exclusionary language; for example, service representative was referred to as "he" while lineman became "linewomen." Results, indicating interest in the traditional opposite-sex jobs, were as follows:

Language Form	Women	Men
Traditional exclusionary	5%	30%
Inclusionary	25	75
Sex-reversed exclusionary	45	65

Since the only difference in these ads was the language used, the conclusion that the generic is interpreted as exclusionary by many people, both male and female, seems inescapable.

Harrison and Passero (1975) investigated the extent to which third graders included females in their interpretations of traditional generic terms. Eight situations were presented; below each were four or five figure drawings. Students could circle the appropriate drawing or drawings. The test was given in two forms; one using traditional generic terms and the other neutral terms such as people, salesperson, handmade. When the traditional exclusionary language was used, 49-85 percent of the students circled male figures only. However, when neutral terms were used only 3-31 percent of the students circled all males. These values were significantly different. The authors concluded that for these children, females generally are not included within their understanding of the traditional generic terms.

Harrison (1975) had more than 500 junior high students respond to seven situations by drawing figures and giving them first names. Three forms were used: Form I (traditional generic): "Draw three examples of early man and the tools you think he used in daily life"; Form II inclusionary terms): ". . .people. . .they. . ."; and Form III (specifically inclusionary): ". . .men and women. . .they. . ." Significant differences were found for both male and female students.

Range of Percentages of Male and Female Students Drawing Only Male Figures on Seven Items

	Male	Female
Traditional generic	49–93%	11–58%
Inclusionary	22–70	5–43
Specifically inclusionary	6–64	2–17

Percent All Male Figures Drawn

	Male	Female
Traditional generic	42%	9%
Inclusionary	17	2
Specifically inclusionary	2	1

Not one student responded by drawing all females for every item. Also a significantly greater number of males than females drew all male figures. The author concluded that the results indicated the effectiveness of traditional generic usage in excluding females.

At seven grade levels (preschool through college) 418 students were presented with statements containing either an exclusionary or inclusionary term by Ernst (1977). Two response formats (free and forced-choice) were used to measure each of three generic word types: traditional generic pronouns, traditional generic nouns, and inclusionary nouns. For the forced-choice format, stick figure illustrations were used and students selected one representing their mental picture of the statement. For free-response, students gave a name to the person described and answered a question about the situation.

"A driver who tried to open his car door"

- Give the driver a first and last name.
- What kind of car was it?

Ernst found that with the free and the forced-choice formats there were significantly more masculine responses for the traditional generic pronouns and nouns, while for both formats there were significantly more feminine responses for the inclusionary noun format than for the traditional generic nouns. The forced-choice format elicited significantly more feminine responses than did the free-response format for all three comparisons. The author concluded that for equal treatment and opportunity for all, there is clear evidence of the need to use inclusionary forms.

Based on this research the following conclusions are reached:

1. These studies are remarkably consistent in their findings.
2. They all agree that when traditional generic pronouns and/or nouns are used, the antecedent is more likely to be interpreted as male.
3. The studies which investigated the effect of inclusionary language found that it significantly decreased the difference between feminine and masculine responses.
4. The study by Ernst implies that inclusionary language alone is not as effective in increasing the inclusion of females as when it is used with pictures (reminders) of females.

Besides this strong research evidence, there are three other considerations. First, it is known that young children react literally to language; thus traditional language constantly shapes and reinforces the concept that boys are supposed to be in certain occupations, while girls are not. At best, traditional language fails to contradict the exclusionary concept while it does serve to reinforce it.

Second, exclusionary language is inefficient and at times misleading. It is not always clear if a term is being used in a generic sense: for example, "This book is about the history of black men in America." At other times, it appears to be generic, but there is a switch later within the sentence to the specific: for example, "The average American does not himself manufacture most of the things his wife and children need."

Third, many occupational terms are improved by becoming better descriptors when inclusionary language is used. Examples include firefighter, garbage collector, and groundskeeper.

Based on the research evidence and these final three considerations, there can be only one logical answer to the original question. Yes, there are implications regarding traditional language usage, beyond mere preference, which ought to be taken seriously by educators.

Specific guidelines for inclusionary language have been developed by a number of publishers and national organizations. In general they suggest substituting other terms for the "man" terms and avoiding the generic use of he and his by pluralizing, by using the expression "his/her" or "her/his" or by rewriting the sentence.

The research reviewed above strongly indicates two needs: (1) The need to use inclusionary language, for example, repair worker. (2) The need to include women specifically by using both masculine and feminine terms such as "he and she," "women and men," "his/her and she/he." Educators, at all levels, who wish to affirm every individual and to encourage equal educational opportunity, will begin by modeling the use of inclusionary language in their speech and written materials.

Images of Males and Females in Elementary School Textbooks in Five Subject Areas

By Lenore J. Weitzman and Diane Rizzo

Despite recent technological advances the textbook remains a cornerstone for our educational system. The textbook represents the officially prescribed body of knowledge which the school-age child is to master. It is thus an important and unique authority for a young child.

Although the primary function of textbooks is to convey information about a specific subject area, textbooks also attempt to instruct the child in ethical and moral values. They portray what is good, desirable, and just. They provide the child with a vision of the future and aid him or her in establishing personal goals for the future. Thus, at the same time that a child is learning history and mathematics, books are also influencing values and aspirations. The results are that textbooks actually provide two distinct forms of knowledge to the young reader. The first kind of knowledge consists of information and skills in a specific subject. The second kind of information consists of ethical prescriptions, a vision of the good life, and the motivations and incentives to attain it.

This second type of information, what sociologists refer to as the "latent content" of textbooks, also conveys images of appropriate male and female behavior. Textbooks provide norms and standards for how men, women, boys, and girls should act. This research report focuses on the latent content of textbooks: it examines and analyzes the ways the two sexes are portrayed and the types of behavior encouraged for each.

The object of this research was to systematically analyze the textbooks being used in the average classrooms in the United States today in grades 1 through 6. Instead of examining the current best sellers, or the most innovative books, we sought to sample books that had been used in most schools during the past five years. In this way we hoped that our study would reflect the situation in the typical classroom in the United States, not just the avant-garde in education. An expert panel of educators and publishers was consulted to determine the most widely used textbooks over a five-year period[1] in science, mathematics, reading, spelling, and social studies.[2]

The major focus of this analysis was the textbook illustrations, as they provided a single uniform indicator with which to compare the different series. Each person in each illustration was categorized along 50 different dimensions including age, sex, race, expression, activity, and occupation. The coded data provided the basis for a systematic analysis of the representation of males and females, as well as the differences by grade level and subject area.

In examining the people in the world of textbooks, three major classifications were used: age, race, and sex.

With regard to age, we found that the majority of the pictures, 57 percent, are children, while adults are 43 percent. The large number of children in the illustrations makes it easier for a child to identify with the pictures and, therefore, to assimilate the lesson.

However, the higher the grade level, the larger the percentage of adults. While adults are only 28 percent of the pictures in the first grade, by the sixth grade they are 73 percent of the total. Thus the textbook world shifts from the world of the child to the world of the adult. And, as the child grows older, he or she is also supposed to shift to adult role models—to imagine the self as an adult and to learn what behavior is appropriate for an adult.

With regard to race, we found that the textbook world is primarily a white world. Whites are 81 percent of the illustrations, while only 8 percent are black, and even fewer are American Indian, Latin, Chicano, or Asian. This underrepresentation of minorities means that the minority child is more likely to feel excluded—and will have more difficulty in identifying with the textbook characters. In addition, all children are deprived of a well-founded picture of our society.

As with age, the proportion of minority persons changes with the grade level of the textbook. In each series the proportion of minority persons decreases as the grade level of the textbooks increases. Thus 33 percent of the illustrations are of minority persons in the first grade, but this decreases to 26 percent by the sixth grade. In math the percentage of minority persons declines from 25 to 15 percent; and in science from 11 to 8 percent. Thus with each successive year, in each series, nonwhites are increasingly excluded from the world of textbooks.

Since women comprise 53 percent of the U.S. population, one might logically expect half of the illustrations to be female. However, females are only 31 percent of the textbook total—while males are 69 percent. Of the total of over 8,000 pictures analyzed, more than 5,500 are male. Males overwhelmingly predominate.

The percentage of females varies by grade level. They are 32 percent in the second grade but decline to only 20 percent by the sixth grade.

This means that by the sixth grade there are four pictures of males for every one picture of a female. The percentage of males, in contrast, increases with each grade level. As a greater proportion of the pictures become adults, women become less numerous, and by implication, less important as role models.

This declining representation of females is particularly striking in

Barbie & Action Man!

some of the series. For example, in spelling, 43 percent are females in the second grade, but by the time we reach the sixth grade the percentage has declined to a mere 15 percent. In science, it drops from 36 to 18 percent.

When we combine the sex and race categories, we find that minority females are doubly disadvantaged. There are only half as many minority females as minority males.

In summary, the data indicate that the textbook world is a world of white males, and as the textbooks increase in sophistication, with each grade level, they become increasingly adult-oriented, and women become increasingly invisible.

It is difficult to understand the impact that these pictures have on children without examining the illustrations themselves. However, several statistically significant differences in the illustrations should be noted.

In the pictures of children, there is a strong contrast between the activities of boys and girls. First, the world of boys is one of action and energy. In contrast, girls are typically shown as passive, watching and waiting for boys. Second, most boys are shown outdoors while a greater percentage of girls are shown indoors.

A third difference is in the traits encouraged in boys and girls. Boys are encouraged to be skillful and adventurous. In contrast, girls are encouraged to pursue homemaking and grooming. Throughout the textbooks girls are shown in domestic roles doing household chores, caring for others, helping their mothers, sewing, baking, mopping, making beds, dusting, and washing dishes. One message for a young girl is that she should learn to help, care for, and serve others.

Girls are also encouraged to make themselves attractive: they are shown combing their hair, trying on clothes, shopping for pretty things, sitting under the hair dryer, and being rewarded for their attractiveness. It is clear that feminine success is reserved for the pretty girl.

These pictures project the message that success for girls will lie in serving, pleasing, and watching others, while success for boys will result from independence and activity. If a little girl identifies with pictures of girls in the texts, she will be assimilating a lesson of subservience and passivity. At the same time the little boy is learning to express independence and creativity.

A fourth difference in the images of boys and girls is in their emotional expression. Girls express a much wider range of emotions. They are affectionate and often shown hugging and nurturing pets and dolls. Girls also frighten easily and are often shown crying. In contrast, boys almost never cry, and the young boy is taught that to be a man he must control his emotions. Thus, in the same way that girls are constrained by images which stereotype them as passive, boys are constrained by images which stereotype them as strong and silent. The textbooks thereby encourage both boys and girls to limit themselves—to be less than full human beings.

Finally, it is interesting to note that in a significant minority of the illustrations with both boys and girls, most of the action centers around boys. Boys act, and girls watch. Often the girls seem thrilled just to watch the boys perform.

An examination of the images of adults in textbooks indicates that the adult world is a world of men. Men are shown in over 150 occupational roles—they are doctors, chefs, farmers, chemists, waiters, carpenters, pilots, etc. The illustrations of adult men are glamorous and exciting—and they stimulate young boys to dream about a wide range of occupational choices.

In contrast, choice is almost nonexistent for girls because the adult women in textbooks are all the same. Although adult women in our society do many things, almost all the women in textbooks are housewives.

The housewife in textbooks is hard to believe: she has little to do, everything goes smoothly, and she is always happy and calm. The reality and difficulties of managing a household (juggling the demands of husband, children, cleaning, cooking, shopping, laundry, entertaining, bookkeeping) and the many important volunteer activities of housewives should be discussed so that both boys and girls can understand their mother's complicated role.

Although the textbook housewife seems artificial, the image of mothers in textbooks is consistently positive—in fact, it is the most positive female image in textbooks.[3] Mothers are appreciated and loved, and there is a very warm and happy bond between mothers and their children. The problem is that motherhood is presented as the only option for girls— motherhood is shown as a fulltime lifetime occupation. But, in reality, the average woman in the United States spends only one-third of her adult years raising children. Most women will want to work outside the home— or will have to work because of economic necessity—in the other two-thirds of their adult years. If our daughters are told to think only of motherhood in their futures, they will not develop the skills they will need for two-thirds of their lives.

Today, 42 percent of the United States labor force is female. In fact, 90 percent of all women in this country work outside their home at some point in their lives. One of the most frustrating experiences of working women is discovering too late that they don't have the skills or training they need for the jobs they want—or the jobs that pay well. And yet, the textbooks are encouraging the same mistake in our daughters. It is totally inaccurate to portray motherhood and work as mutually exclusive. Most girls will want both. The educational system is thwarting and simply cheating our daughters if it doesn't provide them with the skills and aspirations for both.

Although most textbook women are confined to their homes, a few are shown working. They are teachers, librarians, salesclerks, and nurses. Thus, girls' occupational choices, when they exist at all, are severely limited.

In contrast, by providing boys with over 150 occupational choices, the textbooks encourage young boys to imagine themselves in a wide variety of roles—and to dream of becoming anything from a laborer to a doctor.

While boys learn that an exciting future awaits them, the implicit message may also be a heavy responsibility. It is clear that men must have jobs. In fact, all men seem to do is work. This overwhelming occupational focus—and the frenetic activity encouraged in boys—may be what leads to so many ulcers and heart attacks in adult men. The death rate from heart attacks among men in the prime of their lives is four times as high as it is for women—and yet the textbooks seem to be stimulating the same hyperactivity in young boys.

Boys who are pressured to think only of work are being constrained in the same way as girls who are told to think only of motherhood. To confine either sex to stereotyped roles is to arbitrarily restrict their individual talents.

There are systematic differences in the treatment that women receive in the different subject areas. The percentage of women varies from a high of 33 percent in social studies to a low of 26 percent in science. These differences, although they may not appear to be dramatic, are important in understanding why children like certain subjects and want to major in them—or why, in contrast, they may feel unwelcome or excluded because of the covert messages they receive.

In science, the most male-oriented series, three out of every four pictures are males. Throughout the science series the textbooks seem to imply that females have no place in the world of science.

For example, when we open the first-grade science textbook, on the very first page we are told that we are going to learn about making things move. Immediately we learn it is boys who make things move. The next few pictures show boys riding bicycles and pushing objects. The following page contains a picture of a girl and movement, but here we find that the wind is propelling her balloon. It is clear she has no control over the movement of the balloon. The boy on the same page is throwing his basketball. This contrast continues throughout the series. When boys are shown, they are actively involved in experiments: looking through microscopes, pouring chemicals, and experimenting. Boys control the action, and it is they who demonstrate scientific principles of motion, growth, energy, and light.

In contrast, when girls are shown, they observe. They are shown smelling soap and perfume, and looking at rocks, thermometers, and their sunburns. In some pictures girls are used as the objects of experiments, being injured or having balls thrown at them.

Adult women fare even worse than girls do in the science series. While girls are only 20 percent of the total illustrations, adult women are a mere 6 percent. In some grades, such as the second-grade science book, the percentage of adult women is as low as 1 percent. This means that in the second-grade science book, there are no adult women in 99 out of every 100 pictures.

Although our knowledge of women in science is terribly incomplete—because of the burdens they have had in gaining recognition for their work—at a minimum the science books could mention Madame Curie or Mary Leaky. Instead, science textbooks give children the impression that no woman has—or can—play a role in building our scientific knowledge. The scientific world is presented as a masculine domain: all scientists are male, only men do scientific work. The epitome of the male prototype in science is the romantic emphasis on the astronaut. But, once again, it is only boys who are shown in astronaut costumes and in the text only boys are told to imagine that they can explore the moon.

In the mathematics textbooks most males are shown as mathematically competent, but some of the females have difficulty with simple addition and are shown as baffled by counting to three or 20. These "dumb girl" images are not only derogatory and insulting to a girl student trying to learn mathematics—but they clearly contradict reality, for girls do better than boys in mathematics in elementary school. Adult women are also stereotyped: they deal only with math problems of dividing pies and shopping, and some are portrayed as mathematically incompetent. It seems ironic that housewives—who use so much math in balancing bank accounts and managing household budgets—are shown as baffled by simple addition.

Another feature of the mathematics textbooks is the frequent use of sex as a category for dividing people. For example, in explaining set theory, girls are set off as people who sew and cry. When sex is used as a category, girls are told that they can be classified as different—as typically emotional or domestic.

There is also strong sex-stereotyping in the examples and math problems. Despite the Equal Pay Act of 1963 we found math problems in which girls were paid less than boys for the same work. It would be hard to imagine a textbook publisher allowing this example if a black boy was being paid less than a white boy.

In the reading series, story titles provide a good indicator of the relative importance of males and females. Boys predominate in every grade. We see that in total, there are 102 stories about boys, while only 35 are about girls. When we examine the stories, we find that even the female heroines reinforce the traditional female roles. For example, Kirsten, the heroine of a third-grade story, surprises the girls who have rejected her by making Danish cookies and having the most popular booth at the school fair. The moral in this story is that girls can succeed by cooking and serving others.

But Kirsten slights herself and the very skill that has earned her favor. She says: "It's easy; even I can do it and you know how stupid I am." Thus, even when girls succeed, they tend to deprecate themselves.

In contrast, boys show a great deal of confidence and camaraderie. Among both boys and men, pride and male bonds are very strong.

In reading textbooks there are two kinds of roles in which females predominate. Although they are only a small percentage of the pictures, they are significant. First, more women than men are shown as mean or evil characters. It is women who are overrepresented among the witches and villains of the textbooks. By representing evil characters as women, the textbooks further reinforce the secondary status that women are accorded.

The second role in which there are more females than males is among people who are shown as clumsy or stupid, and as the foolish objects of a joke.

26

The antagonism toward women is even more pronounced in the spelling series. In the early spelling books the vowels are shown as females and the consonants are shown as males. Although one might expect statements about how necessary vowels are, or how we can't make words without them, instead the female vowels are treated in an antagonistic and derogatory manner. In the dialogue women are yelled at, kicked out, pushed around, used as puppets, and told to shut up.

The last series, social studies, is unique in several ways. It is the only series with a strong family orientation, and it has the largest percentage of females. Here, mothers are shown as skillful, and they play an important role in passing on their cultural tradition to their daughters. There are many pictures of mothers in other cultures teaching their daughters specific skills.

The social studies series is also unique in its presentation of men in a parental role. There are many warm and tender pictures of fathers and sons; fathers instruct their sons in specific vocational skills—as well as in the ways of life.

Although we applaud these pictures of fathers and sons, it should be noted that fathers teach their sons—but not their daughters. Similarly, mothers teach only their daughters. Thus, once again boys learn vocational skills and girls learn domestic skills. Because the two sexes are segregated, and each sex learns a limited range of skills, traditional sex roles are perpetuated. Today, boys need to learn to manage in the home and to be parents, and girls need to learn about vocations and the outdoors. Again the textbooks could expand rather than thwart the children's potential.

The social studies series is also unique in its presentation of racial and ethnic minorities and the attention it gives to people of other cultures. The percentage of minorities varies by series—from a low of 10 percent in science to a high of 44 percent in social studies. Social studies is by far the best series in its representation of nonwhite and minority persons. The large number of blacks in this series demonstrates that pressure against textbook publishers can have some effect.

However, it is disappointing to note that publishers have not yet made the same effort with regard to women. Although this series has the largest percentage of females in pictures, still two out of every three are male. Once we move away from the home, we find that women are absent from the discussion of history, government, and society. The ways of life are still portrayed as "The Ways of Man."

After studying these textbooks for two years, we cannot help but conclude that our children are being crippled by the latent messages in their textbooks. Why not examine the textbooks you use again: count the number of males and females in the first hundred pages and examine the ways in which each sex is stereotyped. We urge you to examine the textbooks yourselves because only you can change the impact that these textbooks will have on our daughters and our sons and on the next generation of adults.

The Resource Center on Sex Roles in Education has developed suggestions for what students, teachers, teacher groups, administrators, parents, and community groups can do to counteract the covert messages in textbooks.

What is most sorely lacking in the textbooks, and thus most desperately needed in the classroom, is a new image of adult women and a wide range of adult role models for young girls. Both girls and boys should learn about the history of women in this country; about women's suffrage, and the current women's liberation movement and struggle for equality; and about the female heroines of our country and our world. Girls of all racial and ethnic minority groups need to understand the roles that their foremothers have played in the development of our society. What a difference it would make if young girls could point to adult women with pride—and feel that they had an exciting life ahead. This is an imperative for our children, ourselves, and our society.

Sexual Stereotyping and Mathematics Learning

By Elizabeth Fennema and Julia A. Sherman

Although many questions are being asked about the teaching of "modern mathematics," two important ones are seldom asked: Is modern mathematics teaching providing equal opportunity for both boys and girls to learn mathematics, and if not, why not? This paper attempts to provide a partial answer to the first question and a viable hypothesis concerning the second.

The exploration of sex-related differences in mathematics is not new, since sex has been used as a variable in many studies investigating mathematics learning. Reviews of such literature that appeared before 1974 concluded that while there might not be a sex-related difference in young children, male superiority was evident by the time learners reached upper elementary or junior high school. In addition, males were definitely superior in higher-level cognitive tasks, which assume increasing importance as one progresses to advanced mathematical study—algebra, geometry, and beyond.

The reviews of sex-related differences in mathematics published since 1974 do not always draw the conclusion of male superiority in mathematics. Fennema (1974) reviewed 36 studies and concluded that there were no sex-related differences in elementary school children's mathematics achievement. She also found little evidence that such differences exist in high school learners. However, there was a trend for males to excel in higher-level cognitive tasks and females, in lower-level cognitive tasks.

In an extensive study conducted from 1974 through 1976, Fennema and Sherman found minimal sex-related differences in mathematics achievement in grades 6 through 8, and in only half of the high schools studied did males achieve at higher levels than females (Fennema and Sherman 1976[a] and [b]).

The National Assessment of Educational Progress (NAEP) has also reported recently on sex-related differences in mathematics achievement. One sentence in particular has been widely quoted: "In the mathematics assessment, the advantage displayed by males, particularly at the older ages, can only be described as over-whelming" (Mullis 1975, p. 7). Inspection of this data confirms that males did outperform females at ages

17 and 26 through 35. On the other hand, at ages nine and 13, differences were minimal and sometimes in favor of females. Besides the problem of an overgeneralization of results, one other serious problem with the NAEP conclusion about male superiority must be considered. The population sample used was selected with no control for educational or mathematical background. Since males have traditionally studied mathematics more years than females have, a population of males with more background in mathematics was being compared with a population of females with less background in mathematics. At ages nine and 13, when the educational and mathematical backgrounds were similar, the achievement of both sexes was also similar.

Although the belief that males always perform at higher mathematical levels than females is not as strong as it once was, it is still a fact that females elect not to study mathematics in high schools and universities in much greater numbers than males. This choice not to study mathematics severely handicaps females. The Carnegie Commission of Higher Education in *Opportunities for Women in Higher Education* emphasizes that pre-college mathematical training for women is inadequate, and they believe that one of the main barriers that prohibits the advancement of women in today's society is poor mathematical training (Carnegie Commission 1973).

Although the validity of the belief of male superiority in mathematical achievement is being questioned, it appears clear that a problem does exist concerning females' studying of mathematics. Not so clear, however, is why the problem exists. It had been suggested (Stafford 1972) that quantitative ability is transmitted as a recessive characteristic on the X chromosome. If one accepted this hypothesis, it follows that fewer females are inherently as capable as males to learn mathematics. Recent data and analyses, however, do not confirm Stafford's X-linked, recessive hypothesis of the inheritance of quantitative ability (Sherman and Fennema 1976; Williams 1975).

Whether the inheritability of the quantitative ability is important or not appears academic. The inheritance of quantitative ability as an explanation of females' less adequate mathematical performance appears only to be of theoretical interest for at least two reasons. First, the best predictors of success in mathematics are previous mathematical learning and scores on intelligence tests. Since there are no significant sex differences on intelligence test scores and, until about puberty, no significant differences in mathematical achievement scores, the number of females who have equal capability with males for learning high school mathematics is much larger than the number of females who elect to study mathematics in late high school and college. Second, even considering the differences found in male-female average mathematical performance, the performance distributions are not nearly as different as the distribution of the sexes in mathematics/science careers. Clearly, factors other than those associated with heredity must be affecting females' mathematics learning and usage.

One important factor that appears to be affecting females' studying of mathematics is the societal stereotyping of the learning and usage of mathematics as masculine. The hypothesis set forth in this paper is that because mathematics is perceived as a male domain, females sometimes do not achieve as well and tend not to elect to study mathematics to the same degree as they would if it were seen as a neuter domain. Several kinds of evidence give credence to this hypothesis.

During adolescence, when the gap in boys' and girls' mathematical performance becomes increasingly evident, the most salient developmental task is establishing an appropriate sexual identity. There are several indications that the studying of mathematics is linked to this developing sexual identity. Achievement orientation, or the motivation to learn, is likely to be strongest in academic areas that represent culturally defined sex-appropriate activities (Stein and Bailey 1973). Females identify mathematics as a male activity (Stein and Smithells 1969) during adolescence and as a result tend to lack achievement motivation in this area. Not only do many girls not see the learning of mathematics as an appropriate activity, they also do not recognize the usefulness of mathematics to their life plans (Hilton and Berglünd 1971). Lacking high achievement motivation and seeing no relevancy of mathematics to an individual's future life are two strong forces that, if they didn't actively discourage girls from learning, would certainly not encourage girls to put forth much effort in learning mathematics.

Another powerful force that appears to operate differently on boys and girls is parents. Parents perceive mathematics to be more appropriate for boys than for girls, and by their actions parents offer more encouragement to boys than to girls to learn mathematics. Parents report buying more mathematical games for boys (Hilton and Berglünd 1971) and offering more explicit reward and reinforcement to their sons to learn mathematics than to their daughters (Astin 1974).

Although the preceding types of data offer the most direct evidence that girls' election of mathematics courses is related to sexual stereotyping of mathematics as a male domain, there are other indicators of this as well. Females often feel inadequate in many kinds of problem-solving activities (Kagan 1964). As a group, females are more apt to underestimate their intellectual activities in general (Maccoby and Jacklin 1973) and their own mathematical problem-solving ability in particular (Crandall, et al. 1962). This lack of confidence in one's own problem-solving ability is certainly not unrelated to lower achievement orientation. If a person has confidence in his or her own ability within a specified area, then that person is much more apt to be motivated to achieve in that area.

Although low mathematical self-concept interferes with both the ability to learn mathematics and mathematical achievement motivation, it also could interfere with the amount of time spent studying mathematics. (Hilton and Berglünd 1971). There is evidence that boys tend to read more books and magazines concerned with science (and therefore with mathematics) and to talk about scientific topics more than girls do.

Horner's (1972) data and her interpretation of it as indicating that females have a motive to avoid success has been widely publicized. She concludes that females have such a motive that acts as a psychological barrier to their achievement, particularly when the achievement is in competition with males and when the achievement area is perceived as being predominantly masculine. Horner also concludes that while this motive operates increasingly during the high school and college years, it also operates most strongly in bright girls motivated to achieve—that pool of girls, in other words, with the most potential for success in learning mathematics. The Motive to Avoid Success hypothesis seems to be extremely valid in the mathematical area, in as much as all Horner's criteria of areas in which females avoid success fits mathematics—competition with males and an identified masculine area. Mathematics is perceived to be a masculine area and girls tend to become somewhat uncomfortable about competing in a masculine area (Astin 1974).

One intellectual area that may be related to mathematics learning is spatial visualization, although the nature and extent of that relationship is not clear (Fennema 1974). Females do perform at lower levels than males on tests of spatial visualization (Fennema 1974), and less adequate development of this ability may partially explain females' lower performance in mathematics (Sherman 1967). However, even development of spatial visualization skills may be closely related to sexual stereotypes held by our society. Piagetian scholars believe that all cognitive abilities (including spatial visualization) are developed by physical interaction with the environment. Play activities of young children are closely identified with sexual stereotypes of what is appropriate. Sherman (1967) has suggested that boys' interactions with the environment are more apt to involve spatial activities than are girls'. Therefore, even if the intellectual area of spatial ability is a determinant of mathematical learning, it may also be related to stereotypic sex role behavior.

There is, then, an accumulation of evidence that points to the conclusion that sexual stereotyping of mathematics as a male domain operates through a myriad of subtle influences from peer to parent and within the girl herself to result eventually in the fulfillment of the stereotyped expectation of a "female head that's not much for figures." It is in the operation of these subtly intertwined factors that one must look for the development of a course of remedial action.

Why Don't Girls Misbehave More Than Boys in School?

By Daniel Linden Duke

Introduction

Many people who work in or study schools have noted the increasing concern over student behavior and school discipline. Reports of flagrant disrespect for authority, chronic absenteeism, and drug use abound. A congressional subcommittee has even probed the increase in school violence. In all the discussions related to student misbehavior, however, little is heard that pertains specifically to girls. Those who debate, chronicle, and confront misbehavior in schools seem to assume that the problems result primarily from the actions of boys. This article is an effort to investigate the validity of such an assumption and to describe certain issues relevant to the study of girls' misbehavior in schools.

How Do Girls' Problems Compare to Boys' Problems?

As early as the first years of elementary school some girls manifest problems in school. In a longitudinal study at the University of Colorado School of Medicine, male and female future delinquents were matched with nondelinquents (Conger, 1973). Future delinquents of both sexes evidenced poorer adjustment socially, emotionally, and academically. Such girls were less poised, less cheerful, and less friendly than nondelinquent girls. They also demonstrated less respect for authority and for school rules. Of particular interest was the finding that negative affect (unhappiness, moodiness, humorlessness, and discouragement) differentiated significantly for girls, but not for boys. Contrarily, leadership ability differentiated delinquent and nondelinquent boys, but not girls.

The later elementary and junior high years during which most girls begin to mature physically appear to be a critical point psychologically as well. Peterson (1961) found that throughout middle childhood boys consistently displayed more severe conduct disturbances than girls, but that around the end of elementary school girls started to experience more problems than boys. Albert and Beck (1975) administered the Beck Depression Inventory to students in a parochial junior high school and discovered that girls reported less depression than boys in seventh grade, but greater depression in the eighth grade. Girls also indicated a shift from family to peer confidants by the eighth grade, while boys went from family to no confidants. All students rated "excellent" by their teachers had low depression scores, while those with high depression scores were all rated "poor." This perfect correlation could suggest that teachers' judgments of student quality actually were shaped by their assessment of student mental health (the self-fulfilling prophecy effect).

Several studies using the Mooney Problem Check List (Amos and Washington, 1960; Clements and Delke, 1967; Garrison and Cunningham, 1952) reported that pre-adolescent girls indicated more problems than boys. While the first two studies found that boys expressed more problems in the specific areas of "school" and "money, work, and the future," the last one showed girls outscoring boys in all problem areas. Abel and Gingles (1965) administered the Mooney Problem Check List to 2,500 Nebraska girls in grades 9 and 10. Like Garrison and Cunningham, they found that girls checked more problems related to "adjustment to school work" than any other category. The only problem with the Mooney instrument is its implicit assumption that the number of problems checked is indicative of the significance of the problems.

Interestingly, parents also perceived that problems increased as their daughters approached adolescence (Campbell and Cooper, 1975). Using the Walker Problem Behavior Identification Checklist, parents indicated that their adolescent daughters had greater problems with acting out, withdrawal, disturbed peer relations, and immaturity. Only on the distractibility scale did sons outscore daughters.

A recent study of predelinquents in junior high school (Cottle, 1972) suggested that both girls and boys were similarly unhappy with school, a fact that could imply either that (1) the problems expressed by boys and girls in general were becoming more alike or (2) the problems expressed by male and female predelinquents, in particular, were comparable.

Schutz (1958) gave the Billett-Starr Youth Problems Inventory to 500 Florida girls in grades 10 and 11. He discovered three distinct clusters of problems centered, in turn, on general personal anxiety and insecurity, tension concerning relations with others, and difficulties in getting along with parents. Simmons and Rosenberg (1975) found that adolescent girls, particularly whites, had a more unfavorable self-image than boys and tended to be more self-conscious. In addition, they found that white girls were less pleased with their sex role than white boys. Hayes (1943) contended that boys initiated more classroom disturbances than girls, but that girls more often were victimized by these disturbances than boys. An

Australian study (Harper and Collins, 1975) suggested that adolescent problems might vary according to socioeconomic status (SES). Relatively high SES girls, however, reported more problems than high SES boys. Low SES girls suffered the most problems of all groups.

When the literature on juvenile delinquency was reviewed for any data that might help in comparing boys' and girls' problems during adolescence, conflicting findings were discovered. One study (Kratcoski and Kratcoski, 1975) found that the problems which proved upsetting for girls were not as pronounced or influential for boys' behavior. Another study (Stern and Grosz, 1969), though, noted that the personality profiles of delinquent girls and boys were basically the same. Only on two factors, ego strength and self-reliance, did delinquent girls outscore delinquent boys. Presumably, similar personality profiles imply similar perceptions of problems. However, the absence of large-scale systematic research has meant that a clear understanding of the relationship between adolescent problems of boys and girls and delinquent behavior is presently impossible.

The notion that adolescence is a particularly trying period for contemporary girls is underscored also by findings that girls manifest more anxiety than boys (Maccoby, 1966); three-quarters of teenagers who attempt suicide are female (Hofmann, 1975); and rates of delinquency and behavior problems among girls are climbing steadily (Duke and Duke, 1978). Girls reported more internal distress—including tension, depression, guilt, and psychosomatic symptoms—than boys in a recent Michigan study (Gregg, 1976). In fact, the Michigan researchers concluded that high schools were very difficult environments for girls, who had to work harder than boys to achieve similar benefits. Anyone who has been familiar with high school athletics, sex role stereotyping in the curriculum and the counselor's office, and the treatment of pregnant girls by school authorities can only echo the conclusions of the Michigan study.

Juxtaposed against the argument that high school is a more difficult environment for girls than for boys is the fact that girls seem to do better than boys in school (Hampe et al. 1973). Jackson (1968) reported that girls expressed a greater liking for school as early as grades 6 and 7 (though "a greater liking" does not necessarily imply that all or even more girls liked school). Stanton (1974) confirmed this finding for high school girls. *Why do girls find high school more to their liking than do boys when the research suggests that girls have greater problems related to school in particular and adolescence in general?* Several possible explanations, each of which merits further investigation, arise:

1. Girls, in fact, may not have more problems than boys. Boys could simply be less likely to express their problems to researchers. The male peer group seems to propagate the motion that boys are not supposed to care about school and that it is "uncool" to express too many personal problems.
2. Girls may find school more enjoyable than boys because they have fewer nonschool opportunities for satisfaction. While boys tend to voice pleasure in playing sports, working on cars or motorcycles,

and earning money after school, girls do not have as easy access to these activities.

3. Despite the male-oriented nature of school, girls work hard and out-achieve boys in academics, school government, and certain extracurricular activities. Thus, as a result of their diligence and talent, girls would deserve to feel better about school than boys, even though girls also manifest more problems related to school.

Each of these possible explanations lacks much formal research or scholarly attention. Unfortunately, a discussion of them is outside the scope of this article. The real focus of the present study is on another seeming contradiction, one related to the low incidence of reported misbehavior by girls in school.

How Does Girls' Behavior in School Compare to Boys' Behavior?

If it could be assumed that a direct relationship existed between the number of problems an individual perceived or manifested and that individual's behavior, then on the basis of the findings cited earlier there would be reason to hypothesize that girls misbehave more in school than boys. Almost all of the evidence available, however, disputes this hypothesis. *If adolescent girls manifest more problems than adolescent boys, why do boys misbehave more in school than girls?* This question serves as the basis for the remainder of this article.

In speculating on answers to the above question, several possibilities occur:

1. The data on school misbehavior could be erroneous, and girls actually might misbehave as much as, if not more so than, boys. In this event, factors must be found to explain why (a) girls' misbehavior was underreported or (b) boys' misbehavior was overreported.
2. Girls might reserve most of their misconduct for their time away from school, in which case female delinquency would be comparable to or greater than male delinquency.
3. Though girls might manifest more problems, their problems on the whole could be less serious or less criminogenic than boys' problems.
4. Contrary to the basic assumption, no relationship at all might exist between students' problems and their behavior in school.
5. Girls might have more problems than boys and their problems might influence their behavior, but they might possess additional personal characteristics that prevent them from misbehaving as much as boys.
6. Certain external factors (social expectations, prental pressures, teacher biases) intervene in the lives of girls to inhibit their misbehavior more effectively than that of boys.

Each of these six possible answers to the central question will now be discussed.

How Accurate Is the Data on Girls' Misbehavior in School?

The first answer implies that girls appear to misbehave less than boys in school because their misbehavior is not reported accurately. Before addressing the matter of accuracy, though, it might be helpful to review what previous research has said about girls' behavior in general.

Maccoby (1966) included summaries of considerable research on sex differences at the close of *The Development of Sex Differences*. Of 49 studies of aggressive behavior in children and adolescents, boys manifested more aggression than girls in 44. The only areas in which girls seemed to behave comparably to boys was verbal aggression. While it is unclear to what extent aggressive behavior overlaps school behavior problems in general, the former appears likely often to be a component of the latter.

In a California study of behavior problems in young children, Heinstein (1969) provided support for the previous assessment of behavioral sex differences. Even during the preschool years, boys were found to display more oppositional behavior than girls. Girls tended to be more negative and to evidence greater amounts of sensitive and fearful behavior.

Hayes (1943) looked at the classroom disturbances of eighth-grade students and found, among other things, that (1) both boys and girls agreed on what constituted classroom disturbances, and (2) practice teachers reported the same types of disturbances for both boys and girls. Ultimately, however, she concluded that boys initiated a larger number of disturbances than girls. Her conclusion was substantiated by two later studies (Duke, 1976; Zeitlin, 1955). Duke found that only 19 percent of the students identified as chronic behavior problems in a large rural high school were girls. Zeitlin studied behavior problems in Phoenix, Arizona, and reported that girls accounted for less than a third of the problems reported for boys. Of the 12 types of discipline problems Zeitlin studied, girls were found to have higher frequencies only for disobedience, misrepresentation, and cheating. Given the low ratio of girl problems to boy problems, it was indicative of the prevailing belief (in the 1950s) that girls did not misbehave much in school that Zeitlin felt compelled to register great alarm over the significant increase in girls' misbehavior.

Several studies (Gold, 1970; Kratcoski and Kratcoski, 1975) have been made of sex differences related to delinquency. Gold found that, out of 19 types of illegal acts, girls surpassed or equaled boys in perentage of reported transgressions only for running away and hitting parents. Kratcoski and Kratcoski indicated that girls more often than boys ran away from home, defied parental authority, bought or drank alcoholic beverages, and used or sold drugs. The two researchers concluded that "unruly" behavior was becoming more prevalent among girls. Thompson and Lozes (1976) added support to this conclusion by noting that, for the first time, researchers were discovering girls involved in gang delinquency, a domain previously thought to be exclusively male.

To summarize the little research that could be found, girls appear to be misbehaving more than they did previously, while boys continue to hold an edge in most types of misbehavior. Can this conclusion be based on faulty data so that girls actually are misbehaving as much as, if not more so than, boys?

The fact that more research has been conducted on boys' behavior problems in school than on girls' behavior problems creates an impression of greater male misconduct. Several studies even have implied that teachers might report girls' misbehavior inaccurately and enforce rules more strictly and frequently with boys. Serbin and her co-workers (1973) noted that preschool teachers were more likely to take notice of and deal with boys' aggressive behavior than similar behavior by girls. Good and Brophy (1974) observed a tendency for some elementary teachers to be hypercritical of boys. If they do, in fact, harbor different expectations for boys and girls, teachers could report acts of misbehavior more consistently for boys than for girls. Or if teachers are more likely to overlook misbehavior by higher achieving students, then the fact that girls tend to outperform boys in school might account for an overall underreporting of girls' misbehavior.

Hindelang (1976) has argued that youngsters engaging in delinquent acts in groups are more likely to find their way into official court records than those who commit illegal acts alone. He has also noted that urban girls are more likely than other groups to commit illegal acts in the company of others. Hence, it is possible that considerable female delinquency does not get reported.

Gold (1970) has gone further than the previous contentions and maintained that delinquency is underreported for all youth, not just girls. His Flint study and others he cited confirm that at some point in the life of almost every adolescent he or she has acted in a delinquent manner. The problem, according to Gold, is that most delinquent behavior simply never gets recorded anywhere. Official court statistics represent only the iceberg's tip.

In conclusion, it appears that (1) boys generally misbehave more in school than girls; (2) girls misbehave more than boys in certain areas such as cheating; (3) the frequency of girls' misbehavior in and out of school is increasing; and (4) reports of misbehavior are probably inaccurate for girls, in particular, and all adolescents in general. It seems unlikely, then, that inaccurate reporting of girls' misbehavior alone is sufficient to answer the central question.

Do Girls Wait To Misbehave Until They Are Away from School?

If inaccurate data cannot completely explain why girls seem to misbehave less than boys in school, a second hypothesis would be that girls wait to misbehave until they are away from school. Were such an explanation correct, supporting evidence should be available in the research literature and official statistics on delinquency. Despite indications of increasing female delinquency, however, boys still are reported to be more delinquent than girls by at least a 2:1 margin (Duke and Duke, 1978; Gold, 1970). Still unclear is whether the gap between female and male misbehavior is greater in school or out of school.

Traditionally girls often have reacted to certain domestic, school, and social problems by running away or by getting pregnant. Whether such acting out is misbehavior is hotly contested. The important point, however, is that girls did not express their discontent or frustration in the same aggressive or flagrantly illegal ways that boys did. More recently, girls have begun to turn in increasingly larger numbers to alcohol and drugs. Whether the use of these substances can be regarded as substitutes for misbehavior in school is uncertain. It might be speculated, though, that the girls who misbehave in school typically are the ones who also get into trouble away from school. In other words, the net number of misbehaving girls would not be increased significantly by combining the statistics on school misbehavior and out-of-school delinquency. Thus, the hypothesis that girls make up for their good behavior in school by misbehaving away from school is subject to sufficient uncertainty to remove it from consideration as an answer to the central question.

Are Boys' Problems More Criminogenic Than Girls' Problems?

A third possible answer is based on the assumption that girls' problems, though perhaps more numerous than boys' problems, are less serious and less criminogenic (contributory to the development of criminal or delinquent behavior). Unfortunately, few studies have sought to determine whether certain problems, such as depression or fear of failure, are more influential than others in shaping school misbehavior.

If boys' problems centered primarily on academic matters (most studies showed boys did not achieve academically as well as girls) and girls' problems related mostly to social acceptance (as several studies have indicated), it could be hypothesized that boys misbehave more because academic problems lead more to clashes with school personnel than to social problems. It seems reasonable to expect that low achievement more than concern over populatiry might lead to classroom frustration, boredom, incomplete assignments, and negative teacher-student interactions. Silberberg and Silberberg (1971), in fact, cited research that showed aggressive disruptive classroom behavior was related to low achievement. Interestingly, though, their study also noted that low achievement occurred equally among *both* delinquent boys and girls. Thus, while girls in general outperform boys in school, delinquent girls apparently do not evidence greater success than delinquent boys. McPartland and McDill (1976) offered support for Silberberg and Silberberg's conclusions. Analyzing three large surveys of secondary school students, the former authors reported a relationship between the degree to which a student received poor grades and the probability of individual disciplinary offenses in school. The relationship was slightly weaker for girls than for boys, however.

While boys' frustrations over lower achievement in school may lead to more uncooperativeness, disruptive behavior, and challenges to teachers' authority, girls' concerns over social acceptance are likely to produce more friction among peers. Unless such friction has racial or ethnic overtones, it seems doubtful that the squabbling between students, fighting, and character assassination plots which typically result from disputes among peers would be regarded by school officials as major acts of misbehavior. For better or worse, teachers and administrators generally are less disturbed by problems among students than by problems between students and school employees (Duke, 1978).

So far the assumption has been made that the researchers are correct when they conclude that adolescent boys manifest fewer problems than girls. This assumption may not be valid, though. Actually, boys may not only have more serious problems but more total problems as well. One study (Adams, 1964), in which teachers gave boys and girls aged 10-19 questionnaires concerning their biggest personal problem, revealed that boys reported more school (as well as financial) problems than girls. Girls identified interpersonal and family problems as the major sources of their concerns.

Despite Adams' research, most studies continue to suggest that girls experience more school-related problems than boys. What factors might account for this tendency? Boys could be more reluctant than girls to divulge their problems to interviewers or on questionnaires. The adolescent male subculture has downplayed the importance of many school-related problems. Boys who express concern over their classes run the risk of seeming to care too much about school. Alternatively, girls could tend to exaggerate their problems, thus artificially inflating the number of "real" concerns connected with school.

In summary, there is some reason to suspect that boys have more school-related problems than existing research studies suggest. There is also reason to believe that boys' problems, particularly those connected with academic achievement, may contribute more to classroom behavior than corresponding girl's problems. Unfortunately, too little investigation of these issues has been undertaken to warrant the conclusion that girls misbehave less than boys in school because girls' problems are less criminogenic.

Is There a Relationship Between School Related Problems and Misbehavior?

Up to now an assumption has been made that people who manifest more personal problems are more likely to misbehave. Is it possible that no such relationship exists?

For years clinical psychologists and psychiatrists have based many of their interventions on the belief that a direct or indirect link exists between the problems a patient presents and the patient's behavior. Such a belief is so fundamental, in fact, that it is rarely questioned. The literature on the assessment of youngsters with behavior problems is not helpful in clarifying the exact relationship between problems and behavior. Buros (1972), for example, lists a few problem check lists and problem inventories in his compendium of instruments, but few have been validated by systematic observation of the behavior of youngsters who express particular problems. Cottle (1972) did find that responses from junior high school students to problem-oriented statements on the School Interest Inventory were related to delinquent behavior. However, most of the instruments designed to predict delinquency or to identify youngsters with behavior problems have concentrated on factors other than personal problems (Duke and Duke, 1978).

Apparently, many researchers studying adolescent activities have assumed that an individual's problems and his or her behavior are related. Little theoretical discussion of the issue is contained in the literature. A preliminary step to testing the assumption might be to try to reverse it. In other words, on what basis could one argue that an individual's problems and his or her behavior are not related?

It might be argued, for example, that all youngsters have many personal problems during adolescence. Therefore, those who are able to express the most problems may be more aware of their problems and thus more capable of overcoming them than are the youngsters who express relatively few problems. This contention assumes, though, that awareness of personal problems is directly related to success in overcoming these problems.

A second argument could be based on the assumption that the more problems an individual possesses, the less that person is able to misbehave. Such a contention presumes that acts of misbehavior require a certain degree of psychological soundness. Therefore, personal problems would be viewed as inhibitors of misbehavior rather than catalysts.

While provocative, these counterexplanations are too untested to provide much insight into the present discussion. For now, personal problems must be assumed to be potential determinants of behavior (or misbehavior). If adolescent girls manifest greater problems and misbehave less than boys, an explanation probably lies elsewhere.

Do Girls' Personal Characteristics Cause Them To Misbehave Less Than Boys?

Does the possibility exist that girls misbehave less than boys because they are more mature, intact individuals who, despite greater personal problems, can adjust better to the demands of school than their male counterparts? The research findings are confusing.

Some girls' problems, such as those related to sexual activity, may derive from the fact that girls mature faster, both physically and psychologically, than boys. In these instances, maturity constitutes an underlying cause of behavior problems rather than an inhibitor. Researchers too often have assumed that maturity leads to fewer problems rather than more. In any event, recent years have witnessed a softening of adult attitudes toward adolescent sexual activities. These are not considered to be delinquent behavior to the extent that they used to be.

What about other problem areas such as truancy, vandalism, disrespect toward teachers, and classroom disruption? That girls seem to commit fewer of these acts could be attributed to several personal characteristics. The research has shown that girls achieve higher than boys in

41

school. Higher achievement may suggest that girls are more diligent workers (though not necessarily more intelligent). In addition, those who do better in school may have more of a vested interest in obeying school rules.

Research studies have indicated that girls manifest a greater need for affiliation, more positive feelings for others, and less aggressive behavior—personal characteristics that could serve to inhibit antisocial kinds of misbehavior in school (Maccoby, 1966). Even when girls do become aggressive in school, they less often develop into delinquents than aggressive boys (Khleif, 1964). While boys' behavior was found to be affected by watching aggression on television, girls' behavior was not (Stein and Friedrich, 1975). Girls also have been characterized by more moralistic behavior than boys show (Maccoby, 1966). In a study of self-perceptions of ninth-grade students. Wiggins (1973) discovered that girls saw themselves as having better teacher-school relationships, being more competent in a variety of subjects, and having more adequate interpersonal relationships. Boys believed that they had higher levels of academic aspirations and greater competence in sports and science than did girls.

Despite the findings cited above, girls also have been characterised by less positive qualities. Mention was made earlier of their greater tendency to depression and anxiety. Little, however, is known of the exact relationship between school misbehavior and these psychological problems. Does depression or anxiety inhibit or encourage misconduct?

The research on predictors of delinquency suggests that delinquent girls may possess certain personal characteristics not possessed by nondelinquent girls (Duke and Duke, 1978). Lack of self-restraint (Porteus, 1968), withdrawn behavior (Liddle 1958), impulsivity (Ostrov et al. 1972), and low self-concept (Cole et al. 1969) were related to behavior problems. Factors that distinguish delinquent girls from nondelinquent girls do not necessarily account for differences in school misbehavior between girls and boys, however.

Thompson and Lozes (1976) studied female gang members and produced a profile of gang members marked by distrust for authority, a tendency to blame others for problems, and emotional reactions. Stern and Grosz (1969) found that the profiles of delinquent boys and girls were similar, except that the girls scored higher on ego strength and "tough-minded self-reliance." However, the fact that many of the correlates of delinquency are regarded as "masculine" characteristics has served to buttress the impression that *most* girls do not possess the psychological qualities necessary to become serious behavior problems.

The suggestion that girls misbehave less because they are more psychologically sound than boys is an intriguing one, but it ignores the fact that personal characteristcs—both positive and negative—are shaped to some extent by factors external to the individual. It also overlooks the fact that the rates of crime and delinquency for females have been rising faster than the rates for males. Before concluding this discussion, then, it will be necessary to review some of the environmental determinants of girls' behavior.

Do Girls Misbehave Less Than Boys Because of External Factors?

The family, peer group, and school are probably the three most potent external influences on the behavior of the young (with the possible exception of television). If they actually do misbehave less than boys, girls are probably subject to pressures from some or all of these factors.

Family Influences

Kratcoski and Kratcoski (1975) have suggested that family factors together with school failure and sexual involvement account for more female misbehavior than male misbehavior. Male delinquents were reported to be influenced primarily by such factors as rebellion against female authority, a need to assert their manhood, lack of opportunity to pursue legitimate goals, and a desire to emulate adult models. Summarizing considerable research on the family background correlates of female delinquency, Duke and Duke (1978) discovered many conflicting findings. The best "family" predictors appeared to be the mental health of the parents, parents' level of education, the quality of parent-child interactions and parental discipline, and certain special dimensions of mothering. In and of themselves, these factors help account for why some girls misbehave, but not necessarily for why girls misbehave on the average less than boys.

A growing body of literature has suggested that parents bring more pressure to conform to bear on daughters than on sons (Gold, 1970). Parents usually have seemed more tolerant of boys' misbehavior ("boys will be boys"). Boys' emancipation from parental control has tended to be accelerated, while girls have been discouraged from acting independently (Richards, 1966). Accorded less rights to privacy and independent action by parents, girls have found themselves with fewer opportunities to misbehave and greater sanctions when they did. It may be no coincidence that running away from home has been one of the few delinquent acts involving as many, if not more, girls than boys. Should they desire to assert themselves—an act which ultimately can involve misbehavior—many girls have little recourse but to escape entirely from their parents. Boys, on the other hand, have enjoyed more latitude to misbehave while still remaining at home. The argument could be made, in fact, that parental expectations not only serve to reduce the tendency of their daughters to misbehave but also increase the likelihood of misconduct in their sons (Astin, 1975).

Peer Group Influences

Coleman (1961) indicated that adolescence produced a shift in influence away from parents and toward the peer group. Are there aspects of the adolescent peer group, as there are with the family, that may explain why girls misbehave less than boys?

In *The Adolescent Society*, Coleman (1961) noted that a particular group of girls—those from white-collar and better educated families—functioned as the "center of social activities, the center of school activities, and the center of adolescent attention." The fact that these girls in effect controlled the adolescent subculture could only heighten the feeling of being "left out" for girls from different backgrounds (Damico, 1976). Resentment over lack of status and peer attention might well prompt some of these girls to act out. For most girls, though, the desire to be accepted by the "in" group—a group Coleman felt was even legitimized by teachers and administrators—probably acts as an inhibitor for excessive deviant behavior. As with parental expectations, the in group exerts pressure on girls to conform to prevailing norms. These norms rarely include acts of misbehavior by girls (but do not necessarily exclude such acts by boys).

It would be a mistake to think that Coleman's in group represents the entire adolescent subculture. There is, of course, no single peer group, but a variety of groups of teenagers pursuing different goals and behaving in different ways (Cusick, 1973). Some of these groups constitute negative influences on adolescent behavior. Gold and Reimer (1972) reported that girls' use of drugs was much more dependent on their association with boys than *vice versa*. In addition, few girls used drugs when no boys were present. In his Flint study, Gold (1970) also discovered that girls' perceptions of their friends' delinquency was a potent factor in their own delinquency. Girls who perceived their friends as highly delinquent were more than twice as delinquent as girls who did not. Hindelang (1976) found that urban girls, unlike their rural counterparts, committed a substantial number of their delinquent acts in the company of peers. Among the acts most often committed in groups were destruction of property, getting drunk, using force to obtain money or valuables, driving a car while under the influence of drugs or alcohol, and using marijuana. Thompson and Lozes (1976) discovered that girls as well as boys participate in delinquent gangs.

While it is relatively easy to understand how sex-biased parental expectations inhibit girls' misbehavior in school, it is not so clear that the adolescent peer group (or groups) serves a similar function. Recent research seems to suggest that the peer subculture is becoming more of a negative influence on the behavior of both girls and boys.

School Influences

Almost since the beginning of public schooling critics have observed that teachers create many of the problems about which they complain. Teacher expectations, for example, have been linked to low student achievement, the implication being that teachers actually cause poor performance by expecting less from "slow" students (Rist, 1970). Could the so-called self-fulfilling prophecy also be applied to student misbehavior? Might differential teacher expectations or attitudes explain in part why girls are reported for fewer acts of misbehavior in school?

Good and Brophy (1974) noted that elementary teachers, most of whom were women, tended to be more critical of boys. Smith and Greenberg (1975) added that teachers labeled student behavior "appropriate" or "inappropriate" depending on the student's socioeconomic status. The lower the status, the more likely teachers were to accept actions that would have been judged as misconduct for higher status students. This finding, however, did not imply any sex bias—only that teachers possessed different expectations for different students. Serbin and her co-workers (1973), though, did discover that preschool teachers were more likely to respond with loud reprimands and other corrective measures when boys were aggressive than when girls were aggressive. If teachers in later years of schooling continue to overlook misbehavior in girls (and informal observations by the author suggest that they do), this tendency might account for the reports of greater misconduct by boys.

Interestingly, though they may "expect" girls to behave better than boys, teachers do not appear to be any more sensitive to girls' problems. In fact, an argument could be made that the tendency of teachers to overlook girls' misbehavior is indicative of their tendency to overlook girls in general. The argument might proceed as follows. If girls are only going to become housewives when they leave school, why devote much attention to their concerns? Boys, after all, must become breadwinners.

Amos and Washington (1960) found that teachers were relatively insensitive to the problems of junior high school girls. Jackson (1968) cited a study that indicated teachers were more accurate in their perceptions of "dissatisfied" boys and "satisfied" girls than the other two groups. Apparently, the very idea of a "dissatisfied" girl was foreign to many teachers.

Teachers, of course, are not the only influences on student behavior to be found in schools. In an indictment of homogeneous grouping, Kelly (1976) suggested that track position might be the best overall predictor of student attitudes and behavior. Since fewer girls tend to be in lower tracks, this observation could help explain girls' lower frequency of misconduct.

It would appear thus far that two primary reasons why girls misbehave less than boys in school are the expectations and attitudes of parents and of teachers. While the analysis must stop here, ultimately it would be important to investigate why parents and teachers tend to possess sex-biased expectations and attitudes.

Why, for instance, does aggressiveness in girls imply the exercise of leadership or initiative while aggressiveness in boys connotes fighting and belligerence? Is it because girls are not expected to be competitive? Why did one study find that females who committed more aggressive crimes were less physically attractive than other female criminals (Cavior et al. 1975)? What factors present in society account for sex role stereotyping and differential expectations? Why are girls rewarded for compliant behavior while boys are urged to challenge norms? Is the economic system or the prevailing Judeo-Christian value structure at fault? Is there a link between the relatively small number of opportunities for young women and their record of better school behavior? Why, as Duke and Duke (1978) have found, are the correlates of misbehavior different for males and females?

Conclusion

The preceding questions, as well as many others concerning the status of women in the last quarter of the twentieth century, demand and are receiving attention. As for the question that served as the focus for this paper, a satisfactory answer still is wanting. For now, it would seem that girls (1) have more problems (though not necessarily more school-related problems) during adolescence than boys, (2) find that their problems receive less attention from school authorities than do boys' problems, and (3) commit fewer major acts of misbehavior in school than boys. The effort to account for the lower incidence of school misbehavior by girls has produced the following tentative conclusions:

1. The statistics on girls' (as well as boys') misbehavior in school are probably inaccurate, but not to such an extent that this finding can explain why girls appear to misbehave less than boys.
2. Official statistics on delinquency do not support the argument that girls really do misbehave more than boys, but wait to misbehave until they are away from school. Male delinquents still outnumber female delinquents by a 2:1 margin, though the gap is narrowing.
3. Boys probably have more school-related problems than current research reveals, but whether or not their problems are more contributory to school misconduct than girls' problems is unclear.
4. The exact relationship between the number or intensity of an adolescent's problems and his or her behavior is uncertain. It seems likely, however, that an individual's problems in some way influence what he or she does.
5. Girls do possess certain characteristics, such as more compliant behavior and less aggressiveness, that help explain why they misbehave less than boys, but these characteristics seem to be shaped by external factors.
6. The external factors that act to inhibit misbehavior by girls center on the differential (sex biased) expectations and attitudes of parents and teachers, but not necessarily peers.

Whether girls eventually will misbehave as much as boys as a result of efforts to eliminate sex role stereotypes remains to be seen. Early indications are, however, that the incidence of female delinquency, criminal activity, and school misconduct is steadily rising. It would be ironic and distressing, but perhaps expected, that part of the price to be paid for the improvement of women's status is greater female misbehavior. All victories presumably involve sacrifices.

Cutting Sex Bias Out of Voc Ed

By Phyllis Lehmann

Weakened by changing mores and pushed by law, the walls of sex discrimination that long surrounded the nation's vocational education programs have tumbled down. Under the Education Amendments of 1972, schools may no longer bar males from home economics classes or keep females out of shop. Yet, the young woman who wants vocational training in a skilled trade or the young man interested in nursing is still considered something of a freak.

The female high school student who wants to be a plumber, for example, is apt to be discouraged from the start. Her guidance counselor probably tells her about the disadvantages of "man's work." The recruiter from the local vocational school may not take her wishes seriously. She is warned about the employer and union prejudice she may face if she does manage to get through training. And literature from the vocational school reinforces stereotypes by using "he" and "his" when describing a plumber.

In short, the would-be plumber faces sex *bias* in vocational education—an ailment more subtle and often more serious than outright *discrimination*. What's the difference between the two? Amanda Smith of the North Carolina Department of Public Instruction draws an important distinction.

"Sex discrimination is that which is against the law—obvious stuff like unequal pay or outright banning of students from courses," she says. "It's bad, but it's also relatively rare." A school might be in full compliance with the law, she points out, but still have each sex enrolled only in traditional areas because the school has given no thought to the power of sex bias.

According to Smith, "Sex bias is the underlying network of assumptions that says men and women should be different, not only physically, but also in their tastes, talents, and interests. Every one of us is biased, even those of us who are paid not to be."

Sex bias in career education limits choices and opportunities for both sexes. It is largely responsible for the following statistics: Half of the students enrolled in secondary or post-secondary vocational training are female. Yet, the teaching and administrative staffs of vocational schools are overwhelmingly male.

Statistics for 1975, the latest data available indicate that of the young women enrolled in federally assisted vocational training, 37 percent are in home economics. But only 3.8 percent are in the type of home economics training that will prepare them for any job other than housewife. Another 23 percent are in clerical training that prepares them for "women's work"—usually at the bottom of the pay scale. Only 5 percent are enrolled in trade, industrial, or technical training.

"Too many girls are being steered into low-paying jobs or into domestic activities that won't pay a dime—not into plumbing, where they'd get $10 an hour," says Pat Beyea, coordinator of the Women's Rights Project for the American Civil Liberties Union (ACLU). "Not every girl should become a plumber or a carpenter, but she should have the chance to."

The attitude that boys should be encouraged to prepare for certain occupations and girls for others permeates all layers of the vocational education establishment. It is equally ingrained among employers, labor unions, parents, and, to an astonishing degree, young people themselves.

One recent survey of 81 post-secondary vocational schools in 26 States found that most of the 860 women who chose nontraditional training received virtually no support from their schools or guidance counselors— or from other women. Surprisingly, they were encouraged most by male vocational teachers.

Fearing that their children will lose masculinity or femininity, some parents recoil at the thought of their son taking home economics or their daughter learning to be an auto mechanic. Some also deny reality. One woman who speaks to community groups about opening up job options for both sexes has encountered mothers who argue that women don't really need to work. Yet these same mothers spent their entire adult lives working outside the home.

Perhaps the most conservative attitudes are found among the supposed victims of educational sex bias. Peer pressure no doubt has convinced more than one adventurous young woman to shy away from carpentry and prompted many a young man to forget about nursing.

In one program designed to change teen attitudes, Illinois high school students were asked to sketch a person performing a particular job. "When we asked how many drew a man working as a nurse, they looked at us like we were stark raving mad," says Dr. JoAnn Steiger, an educational consultant who specializes in increasing vocational education opportunities for women. Similarly, a Texas study showed that 41 percent of the adults surveyed—but only 17 percent of the students—thought both sexes could be airline pilots. Some experts don't find this stereotyping by youth unusual at all. As Amanda Smith points out, kids have lived in a world of comic books, television, and advertising. Adults, on the other hand, have been around enough to know the exceptions to the stereotypes.

Because of its direct link with employment, vocational education is getting much of the blame for the sex bias that infects job training and recruiting efforts. "Women's jobs have always been undervalued and underpaid compared with men's jobs in similar professions, as in the case of nurses and doctors," says Pat Beyea of the ACLU. "The cause usually can be traced right back to the doors of the vocational education schools."

But Deborah Ashford, special adviser on women's issues to the Deputy Commissioner of Education for Occupational and Adult Education, maintains that although changes in vocational education are coming about slowly. "Voc ed is changing just as rapidly as any other segment of the educational establishment." She says this type of training has simply been scrutinized more closely for sex bias because of the sharp differences in enrollment patterns for females and males.

"Much of the bias has been unintentional," she says. "Vocational education can certainly be critized for being sex biased, but vocational schools should not be asked to assume the full blame for a society that programs children from the day they are born. Voc ed is only a part of a society riddled with sexism."

On the other hand, Ashford notes, vocational schools are a very good place to bring about change, and she is optimistic about the shifts that are taking place. "The state and local people recognize there is a problem and want to help in correcting it."

Others are equally heartened by what they see happening. "There's a long way to go before there will be any real changes in the classroom, but the idea that one's job should not be determined by one's sex is catching on," says JoAnn Steiger. One important recent development at the national level was passage of the Education Amendments of 1976, which go further than ever before in spelling out the responsibility of the states to overcome sex bias in vocational education. The law requires states to specify in detail the action they are taking on sex bias, to provide incentives for local school systems to take similar action, and to hire personnel to monitor success of these efforts.

Some states and individual schools are already making impressive strides toward sex fairness in vocational education. The Texas Department of Public Instruction, for example, has developed a model project on Equal Vocational Education—dubbed Project EVE—to inform young women about the full range of job opportunities and to recruit them for nontraditional training. In a program offered at nine Houston high shools, girls were introduced to nontraditional jobs through a special career day; tours of their own schools' vocational training facilities (which many girls never get to see); a slide show, "All About EVE," that depicts the history of women at work and shows women in nontraditional jobs; and a mini course on how to plan for the future.

"We approached it strictly from an economic point of view," says

Project Director Fredell Bergstrom. "We told them,'You're going to be working for 20 or more years of your life, so why not look at all the options.'"

The results have been impressive. In 1975 only 39 girls were enrolled in nontraditional courses at all nine schools. Last year, the number was estimated to be almost three times higher.

The materials used in Project EVE have been assembled into a manual that tells other schools how to plan their own career days, attractively promote all types of jobs, and get updated information about the labor market. Bergstrom now is working with a Houston community college to develop a six-week course to introduce women at that level to nontraditional jobs.

One of the most gratifying things about Project EVE, Bergstrom says, was the overwhelming supoport of local businesses. Employers contributed $3,000 to convert the "All About EVE" slide presentation into a film that is now sold or rented to local school districts. Some gave women working in nontraditional jobs time off with pay to speak to students about their work. "The shortage of skilled labor is so great in Houston," Bergstrom says, "that hiring is not a matter of sex. Employers need skilled people of either sex."

In North Carolina, the New Pioneers Project to Eliminate Sex Bias in Occupational Education is trying to change attitudes among state voc ed staffers, guidance counselors, and students themselves. Project workshops and conferences introduce educators to the concept of sex stereotyping through a filmstrip. "I'm Glad I'm a She! I'm Glad I'm a He!" The strip traces sex stereotyping from practices like wrapping infants in pink or blue and coaching girls to use tears and boys to use fists to get what they want.

The program, which started in 1974 as a pilot offered at 10 schools, emphasizes the need for both sexes to plan for a lifetime when they choose careers. Boys learn about the rewarding human aspects of fields like nursing or child development, while girls learn that the skilled trades offer women good salaries, the chance for part-time employment, and job opportunities in almost any part of the country.

The changes in vocational enrollments have been encouraging. In the year after the program started, female enrollments increased nearly fourfold in farm production, sixfold in bricklaying, and more than threefold in carpentry. At the same time, male enrollments almost doubled in foods and nutrition and more than doubled in housing and home furnishings.

While the number of students in nontraditional fields is still relatively small, Smith says, "The ones and twos are sometimes more important than the thousands. If we never had a girl in carpentry, and now we have two that's significant." Moreover, she adds, the project is changing attitudes, even among students who stick with traditional fields.

Among students in nontraditional courses, the message has clearly gotten through. Smith recalls chatting with a very feminine looking girl enrolled in an auto mechanics class: "playing the devil's advocate, I said, 'You'll chip your nail polish.' She gave me a gentle smile. 'For the money a mechanic makes, I can buy a lot of nail polish.'"

In Brooklyn, N.Y., Nathan Mayron, principal of Eli Whitney Vocationl High School, booms, "This nonsense about separation of the sexes is ridiculous." In the fall of 1973, Mayron began a unique program requiring all ninth graders—who come from some of the toughest neighborhoods in New York—to spend a month in each of the 10 vocational training areas offered at Whitney.

Boys spend the same amount of time in cosmetology as in electrical installation; girls learn as much about business machine repair as about dressmaking. The theory: When the students reach tenth grade, they will be much better prepared to choose a career on the basis of interest and aptitude rather than according to sex stereotypes. Since everyone is in the same boat, Mayron says, "no one is laughing anymore because there's a boy in business education."

Mayron says student behavior has changed in other important ways. "Boys and girls used to sit in separate areas of the cafeteria," he recalls. "Now there's real togetherness, because they're in the shops together. Their personal appearance has changed. Some boys are even wearing suits and ties."

Mayron is careful to prepare parents for the unusual by inviting them to a special orientation session outlining the school's entire program. This year about a dozen students will graduate in nontraditional areas. Next year two young women graduating in upholstery will receive their union cards as the first female members of the New York Upholsterers' Union.

Numerous other local programs are changing attitudes—and aptitudes—around the country. An exhaustive list compiled by Mary Lovell of the Office of Education's Bureau of Occupational and Adult Education includes the following:

- In Gautier, Miss.,Gulf Coast Junior College is training women as apprentice pipefitters, boilermakers, and sheet metal workers— crafts in demand by the local shipbuilding industry.
- The Southwest Kansas Area Vocational Technical Education School in Dodge City is training women to drive trucks, a skill that will enable them to land high-paying jobs or to work alongside their truckdriver husbands.
- In the District of Columbia, the public school system and the Chesapeake and Potomac Telephone Co. offer a joint program to train girls as phone installers and cable splicers and boys as operators.

To a limited extent, these efforts are showing up in national enrollment figures. The percentage of young women in trade and industrial courses increased from 11.7 percent in 1972 to 12.6 percent in 1975, while the number of boys enrolled in home economics and office and health training courses also increased slightly. Meanwhile, the percentage of girls in all types of home economics courses—those designed for the future housewife as well as those that are job-oriented—declined.

Future statistics will probably continue to reflect a blurring of sex stereotypes in voc ed enrollments, Deborah Ashford believes. But there is still a long way to go, and it may take years for the subtle changes in attitudes now taking place to be reflected in significant numbers.

Ashford believes the issue, though, is not just which sex is preparing for which job, but whether vocational schools are preparing *both* sexes to survive in today's world.

"The problem is greater for females now, but we have to recognize that we have also failed males if they graduate from vocational schools without being prepared for all the aspects of raising a family. Vocational education has been very successful in educating students for half their lives—boys to enter careers, girls to be homemakers. Now we have to start educating them for all their lives."

Assisting the School-to-Work Transition for Young Women: Who Needs the Counseling?

(From *Young Women and Employment: What We Know and Need To Know About the School-to-Work Transition*, U.S. Department of Labor, Office of the Secretary, Women's Bureau, 1978, Mary Ellen Verheyden-Hilliard.)

The kind of transition which a young woman makes from school to work is not determined in the spring of her senior year or through some short-range planning beginning in the junior year. That transition from school to work, its smoothness, its effectiveness, its development into a job with a future to it will, in large measure, be determined by how she is counseled and trained in all the years that went before.

The school-to-work transition will be affected by how much affirmative effort we did or did not put into raising her awareness concerning why financial independence is important for her to maintain.

Why Is It So Hard to Counsel Girls to Financial Independence?

Somehow we have a hard time encouraging girls in elementary and junior high school, and even in senior high, to plan for life-long financial independence in a job that has a future to it. When girls get into high school, we get nervous about what we see looming ahead for most of them—and what we see looming is nothing—so we begin to discuss "something to fall back on." Or if she is already one of this year's 1,000,000 pregnant teenagers, we tend to wring our hands and discuss "back-up support measures."

But to come right out and say to a girl from the day she sets foot in kindergarten—"Listen, plan to be responsible for your life" and back up that statement with chapter and verse of *why* she should be financially responsible for her life seems to be beyond the capability of most people to do. Somehow, it seems almost subversive to educate girls for financial independence.

The Cinderella Syndrome

Probably the reason it is so difficult to educate a girl for independence is because we all suffer from the Cinderella Syndrome, the belief that every girl when she leaves school at whatever age—high school dropout, high school graduate, college graduate, or Ph.D.—is only going to work for a little while until she is discovered by the Prince and carried off to live in the castle (or the apartment as the case may be) where she will be kept busy taking care of the princes and the princesses and she will never need to work or want to work outside the home again. And she and the Prince will live happily ever after, until they are both 100 years old, at which time they will both die on the same day.

We have all heard the statistics as to why educating girls through 10 years of public school without disabusing them of the Cinderella myth is cavalier at best and cruel at worst. The trends are reported in every newspaper every week:

— Almost 50 percent of the American labor force is now made up of women.
— The divorce rate is up 109 percent since 1962 and rising.
— Only one out of five women in divided families receives child support from the fathers.
— Two-thirds of all the old people who are poor are women.

Yet it seems we studiously ignore these facts until it is too late. We not only don't inform our Cinderellas, we often actively encourage them to plan for a life of dependency which will have disasterous results.

Who Needs the Counseling?

To the question "Who Needs the Counseling?" if young women are to make an effective school-to-work transition, one must answer: Practically everybody. Parents, teachers, counselors, school administrators, the girls and young women themselves, their male peers, and the business community all need assistance in recognizing why girls and young women must be seen as potential adult human persons.

Research indicates that although it may be unconscious and non-malicious, counselors do discriminate in their advice to young women and to young men. For example, in a recent study counselors were given a "biography" of different students which indicated sex, a racial identification, information about abilities, interests, attitudes, and I.Q. ratings. The study asked counselors to set out an education program with suggestions for career counseling based on what the biographies revealed. The information collected revealed that while males were counseled toward a higher career than were minority women and men, or non-minority women who had the same IQ, interests, and abilities.

Although biased counseling is a reflection of attitudes in all of education and in society in general, it is also a violation of Title IX of the Education Amendments of 1972 because Title IX says in Section 86.36 that you may not counsel differently on the basis of sex. Furthermore, in Section 86.7 Title IX says you may not be excused from complying just because the *present* status of the job market may provide fewer opportunities for one sex or the other in certain jobs.

Another thread running through the research is that boys and men are less willing than girls and women for women to break out of the stereotypes. The research indicates that boys are less willing than girls for women to have more prestigious jobs, less willing for women to take more part in the important work of the world, and unwilling to do much, if anything, to help women achieve their goals. One survey of Ivy League schools asked unmarried men if they would be willing to change their role "in any way" to help a future wife with her career. Less than 7 percent said they would be willing to change their role *"in any way."*

Parents, too, have different expectations for their daughters than for their sons. For example, parents with sons interested in science support that interest with toys, books, and games. Other research indicates that very few parents noticed when their daughters showed an early interest in math or science. So the socialization begins early as girls learn what brings them rewards and what is ignored.

Business people also need counseling if they are to help young women become independent. For example, those who think training a young woman is a waste of time because she is going to quit and get married are engaging in sex bias, sex stereotyping, and sex discrimination and they need new information about the role of women in the work force. They may also need assistance in working through their own traditional attitudes about the "place" of women.

As it interacts with the business community, a school must also be aware of Title IX responsibilities. A school cannot cooperate in any kind of outside program, work/study, youth program, placement, whatever, if that program is placing people on the basis of sex or is working with employers who hire on the basis of sex. Title IX says that any institution or agency receiving federal financial assistance may not discriminate on the basis of sex or assist others to discriminate on the basis of sex.

An Affirmative Action Childhood

In addition to the counseling necessary to change the attitudes and the behaviors of all those significant others who interact with girls and young women, we must, of course, work with the girls and the young women themselves.

Girls need an Affirmative Action Childhood to counteract external pressures and to begin to change their view of what their lives can be. They need lots of on-going talk and discussion about changing women's roles, about themselves as persons of *importance, worth,* and *dignity* who can be *independent* people. They need lots of affirmative career and vocational programs. They need an educational program which recognizes the need for independence. They need support from their parents and teachers and counselors. And, where necessary, they need support to *deal* with the negative reactions of their parents, teachers, counselors, *and* boys.

Girls need affirmation from the day they set foot in kindergarten that it is all right for a girl to aspire to everything and that it is essential to plan to be an independent woman. Work plans should not be a patch that we rush to sew on a girl's life when she is a senior in high school. Such patchwork, however pretty and decorative, is not going to be as strong as if we had woven the design into the fabric of her life.

My experience tells me that there are a lot of good people out there who simply don't realize what they are doing to girls, and what the terrible long-range human cost will be. Until that situation has changed, the answer to the question "Who Needs the Counseling?" will remain unchanged: Practically everybody.

Enlarging the American Dream

By Donna Hart

Traditionally, American society has been willing to accept culturally different peoples if they in turn were willing to reject their cultural distinctiveness. Assimilation, until the late 1960s, was accepted by almost everyone, educators and large segments of most ethnic communities prominently included. During the past decade, however, an emerging sense of heritage that is being more and more proudly expressed by racial minority and national origin groups is changing all this.

The past definition of education's function—to remodel citizens for conformity to a single homogeneous model of acceptable behavior and beliefs—is being challenged. Many Americans now contend that democratic education should have cultural pluralism as a goal. They argue that the rich cultural mix in America—the different values, customs, traditions, and religions—can expand everyone's horizons as it affects all aspects of life, including sex-role attitudes and issues of concern in education.

This article presents an overview of the impact of the women's movement on cultural norms and heritage and the cultural differences and educational experiences of five minority groups—Puerto Rican, Chicano, Black, Asian, and Native American. Though these five groups by no means represent all minority women, they do indicate the needs of a major segment of minority women as they differ from the needs of Anglo women.

Black Women

Black women, victims of double discrimination because of their race and sex, are often asked to make a choice with regard to their priorities: "Are you black first, or female first?" The plain fact is that they are both and have no way to separate the two. Many black women believe that the effort to *force* a separation of the two, especially as that relates to establishment of society priorities, has worked to the detriment of both the racial movement and the women's movement. The black woman is the victim of both racism and sexism, and therefore represents a potentially powerful unifying force around issues for both movements.

In a piece included in *Voices of the New Feminism*, writer Pauli Murray says, "Because black women have an equal stake in women's liberation and black liberation, they are key figures at the juncture of these two movements. White women feminists are their natural allies in both cases. Their own liberation is linked with the issues that are stirring women today: adequate income maintenance and the elimination of poverty, repeal or reform of abortion laws, a national system of child-care centers, extension of labor standards to workers now excluded, cash maternity benefits as part of a system of social insurance, and the removal of all sex barriers to educational and employment opportunities at all levels. Black women have a special stake in the revolt against the treatment of women primarily as sex objects, for their own history has left them with the scars of the most brutal and degrading aspects of sexual exploitation."

The notion that the black female enjoys a favored economic position in relation to the male is a myth. The belief that black women have always been "liberated," and therefore do not need to be involved in a movement to liberate women is also a myth. The media-produced stereotype of the women's movement as a middle class white woman's struggle to escape from housework and child rearing, to get out of her home and into the job market ignores the black woman who may have been a family breadwinner but who lacked the opportunity to make free choices concerning her life.

Historically, these "breadwinner" jobs have been the result of the economic structure's need for cheap labor. Because of an economic necessity of earning a living to help support the family and a need for the black community to draw heavily upon the resources of all its members in order to survive, black women have taken jobs that few others would accept; thereby they unwittingly aided in creating the myth of the female's dominance in the black family. This illustrates how racism has affected the relationships between black males and females. As black men develop access to the economic power structure, black women for the first time have wife or worker options that many white women have had for a long time.

Diane Slaughter of the University of Chicago, in examining the different adaptive strategies black women have arrived at, suggests, "The strongest conception of womanhood that exists among all pre-adult females is that of the woman who has to take a strong role in the family. They [the pre-adult females] accepted the situation as part of life and tradition in the black community. It is against this backdrop that the symbol of the resourceful woman becomes an influential model in their lives."

As a result of her research, Afro-American sociologist Joyce Ladner sees three primary agents of socialization for the pre-adolescent black female: (1) the immediate and extended family; (2) the peer group; and (3) negative community influences such as exposure to rape, poverty, violence, and the like. The strong personality that results from exposure to the harshness of life enhances the girl's chances for survival and her adequate functioning within society. To "survive," the black woman must "make it" as a mother and a worker.

Consequently, over the years, education has been one of the black movement's priorities. The black woman's aspirations toward education are associated with an emphasis on career possibilities that are seen as making possible or easing the maintenance of the black family.

Despite the faith of black women in the education system as a means for social and economic advancement, equal education has not assured them equal access to opportunity. Black women with degrees equivalent to those held by men and white women have been unable to obtain equivalent jobs. The gap between the salaries of black men and women has widened. Both black and white women with some college education earn less than a black male who has only eight years of education.

Although the black woman has made great strides in recent years in closing the educational gap, she still suffers from inadequate education and training. In 1974, approximately 75 percent of black women had completed high school compared with 85 percent of white women. Although there was a 56 percent increase in college enrollment of blacks between 1970 and 1974, only 16 percent of black women were enrolled in college at the end of that period. A college degree is attained by only 7.6 percent of black women.

Since 1970, little evidence exists of any advance in the relative earnings of black females. A look at the jobs in the top 5 percent of the earnings distribution shows that black females held none of them in 1960 and essentially none in 1973. Black women earn less than white women (a median income of $2,810), are employed in greater numbers (about 60 percent between the ages of 20 and 54), and hold a greater percentage of low-paying, low-status jobs (54 percent are employed as operatives or service workers). In 1975, 35 percent of black families were headed by women who earned a median income of only $4,465. That there is still a large number of black women in the labor force reflects to a considerable degree their continuing obligation to supply a substantial proportion of family income. It also suggests that educational attainments, no matter how small, raise participation rates more for black than for white women.

The quandary of black women is how best to distribute their energies among the multiple barriers of poverty, race, and sex, and what strategies to pursue to minimize conflicting interests and objectives.

More and more, young black women are starting to think about their futures as black women in the United States. They are not accepting societal interpretations of their roles. In the process of thinking things through they are being realistic about the roles that they will embrace. Black women will still have to work, but they want to work at jobs that are more challenging and that more fully use their strengths and talents. They want quality education and training to develop their abilities and interests. They want education that respects cultural differences and that educates for liberation and survival.

Puerto Rican Women

In immigrating to the states, Puerto Ricans differ in one main respect from most other minorities who preceded them: They come as American citizens. Nevertheless, numerous problems—differences in customs, racial inequalities, and a limited knowledge of English among them—have restricted their social, economic, and educational success.

Many Puerto Ricans report that the family, which is very important in traditional Puerto Rican culture, experiences a tremendous shock when it is transplanted from Puerto Rico to the mainland. No role in the Puerto Rican American family has been more challenged by immigration than that of the father. In traditional Puerto Rican culture the man is the undisputed head of the household. Meanwhile, the "good woman" obeys her husband and stays at home, working long hours while caring for the children. But whether head of household or "good woman," the individual subordinates his or her wants and needs to those of the family.

On the United States mainland, where women have more prominence and stature, these traditional Puerto Rican roles are undercut. Puerto Rican women are not shielded from mainland differences. Economic need often projects them into the labor force where they are confronted by the greater expectation of women's roles. Then, too, the school and community teach Puerto Rican children that they should have more freedom, be more aggressive and independent, and should speak English rather than Spanish. These influences change the traditional roles within the family, causing strains, role conflicts, and identity confusion.

The Puerto Rican woman often drops out of school at an early age to enter the labor force (at the lowest level) in the hope that her wages will help her family out of a life of poverty. When she is able to find a job, she faces serious disadvantages, not least among them her lack of knowledge of English and the lack of bilingual programs in her community. Adequate training is another lack that keeps a decent salary out of reach, a situation that further compounds her housing, health, and other problems.

Of no assistance to her plight are discriminating hiring practices that have Puerto Rican women working for a lower wage than Puerto Rican men despite equal pay legislation. Many of the available opportunities have been so-called "women's jobs," which are economically and politically powerless and amount to nothing more than low-paid unskilled drudgery.

Supporting this glum picture of Puerto Rican women in America are the 1975 U.S. Census figures that show 1.7 million Puerto Ricans in the United States, 906,000 of them female, of whom only 154,000 have jobs. More than half of Puerto Rican women participating in the labor force are operative or service workers, and 68 percent of those working earned incomes below $5,000. The most recent data indicate that 31 percent of Puerto Rican households in the United States are headed by women who earn a median income of $3,889.

Puerto Rican women in America complete an average of 9.5 years of school. Only 25 percent of them attain a high school education and a mere 3 percent are college graduates. Their educational attainments, like their employment, are hampered by their imperfect grasp of English and their identity confusion, which is often exacerbated by mainland prejudice and their own sense of being strangers in a foreign country. Of significant concern to Puerto Rican women is how much the lack of access to "mainstream" education influences their social and economic situations.

Puerto Rican women in the United States are still struggling with racial as well as sexual discrimination in housing, education, and hiring. They find the women's movement defined by Anglo-American standards and often oblivious to the special needs and strengths of minority women. They feel that the movement has tended to ignore and obscure the racist issue, resulting in double discrimination for minority women.

Puerto Rican women will not separate themselves from their cultural heritage or be alienated from their men. They strongly support the qualities of womanhood, strong family ties, and respect for the family as an institution. They will accept a movement that confronts sexism, but not one that divides the sexes. If the movement appeals to the issue of basic human rights, to the values inherent in the freedom of both sexes from sexism, and to the proposition that when a woman has freedom of choice this also frees the man—if this, in fact, is the meaning of the women's movement, then many Puerto Rican women will support it.

Mexican-American Women

Mexican-Americans constitute the second largest minority in the United States today, and more than 90 percent of them are city dwellers. Vilma Martinez, a young Chicana (feminine form of Chicano) lawyer, has speculated that "in 15 or 20 years the Hispanic population will surpass the black population. Our citizens must be awakened to the ramifications of this fact: Hispanos are a nationally significant, and not a regional, group."

Historically, the Chicano family has been patriarchal and authoritarian. Economic, social, and political leadership in Chicano communities traditionally has been male-based. Education, sexual liberties, and material comforts have been for the men, with the women taking a subordinate, supportive role within the family. The Chicana was controlled by her parents until she married and then had to be faithful to her husband and children.

Chicanos often place a greater emphasis on the family as a unit than on its individual members. Parents stress the use of Spanish as their children's primary language, insisting that to give up Spanish would be to say that one's ancestors accounted for nothing and that one's culture had made no impression on the history of the Southwest. The feeling prevails that the family nucleus would disintegrate if the children could not speak in Spanish to their grandparents.

Chicana leaders see three distinct choices open to Mexican-American women: The Chicana can adopt the traditional sex role, imitating the rural Mexican woman whose place is in the home; she can choose a dual role in which she is bilingual and begins to move away from traditional religious and family sex-role images; or she can cut her cultural ties and identify with the "liberated" middle class white woman.

This diversity of role models for women within the Chicana community requires special consideration by education policymakers. Chicanas themselves express the need for having specific role models which they can follow at all education levels—elementary, secondary, community college, and higher education. And they're talking about teachers and administrators, not just Chicanas in school cafeterias. Many of them are looking beyond community college training as secretaries or as cosmetologists.

Educational and vocational training opportunities must, therefore, be made more accessible and relevant to Chicanas' lives. The deficiencies in our educational system as it relates to Chicanas are underscored in that Chicanas complete an average of only nine years of school. One-fourth of them have completed less than five years of school, 23 percent have completed high school, and only 2.2 percent of those 25 years of age and older are college graduates.

These low figures do not translate the zeal with which Chicanas seek education despite the many obstacles. One formidable barrier is hydra-headed discrimination because of race, color, national origin, language, and sex-role socialization. Then there are damaging or inadequate counseling, ill-prepared and unmotivated teachers, culturally biased achievement tests, inequality of school finances, tracking into noncollege preparatory courses, economic deprivation, and a lack of role models.

Parents of Chicanas recognize the value of education as a tool for survival in a complex society. They encourage their daughters to pursue education, and there is a sense of family pride about a daughter's attendance at college. But parents also want Chicanas to remember their traditional family values and roles. Thus under pressure to succeed as both student and Chicana within a strange, impersonal, and often inflexible college environment, the young woman becomes vulnerable—and little wonder—to the despair and frustration that account for the high dropout rate of Mexican-American women.

Nor can the economic realities that often preclude interest in and access to educational attainment be overlooked. The annual income of Chicanas in 1974 demonstrates a cycle of poverty, with 76 percent of them earning less than $5,000. In terms of earning power as compared to all other Spanish-origin women, the Chicana is at the bottom, earning a median annual income of $2,682. It must also be noted that Chicanas are increasingly in the labor force because of economic need and responsibility as heads of households; 14 percent of Chicano families are supported by Chicanas, and one-half of these are below the poverty level.

Chicanas have tended to be suspicious of the woman's movement, which came about just as the minority movement was gaining momentum. Hostility toward white women who have moved into the forefront with their "sexual politics" results from the Chicanas feeling that class interests have been obscured by the issue of sex which is easier to substantiate and to deal with than are the complexities of race.

Chicanas, along with many other minority women, question whether or not white women in power positions will perform any differently than their white male predecessors. Will white women work for humanity's benefit? Will they use their power to give entry skills and opportunities to minorities? Chicanas have seen little evidence of white women addressing these broader needs or exhibiting an understanding of the minority-wide issue of redistribution of income levels.

Bea Vasquez Robinson of the National Chicana Coalition succinctly states the minority women's position vis-a-vis the women's movement: "To expect a Chicana who has felt the degradation of racism to embrace a movement that is once more dominated by whites is childish." And in another instance, "We will join forces to the extent that you white women are willing to fight, not for token jobs or frills, but rather go to the roots of our common oppression and struggle for economic equality."

The Chicanas' prime concerns are economic survival and the continuance of their culture. Their issues are broader than sexism; theirs are racism and cultural pluralism as well.

American Indian Women

In any discussion of American Indian women, it is necessary to keep in mind the diversity among the 789 tribal entities existing today. Writing for the *HUD Challenge*, social scientist Regina Holyan says, "Some tribes allow and encourage prominent authoritative behavior on the part of their women, while other tribes such as the Navajo and Cherokee prefer that their women not act conspicuously in decision-making roles. These conflicting expectations by different tribes place Indian women in sensitive situations when they must interact with members of other tribes."

Nonetheless, like the Chicanas, American Indian women may choose among three separate subcultural roles: the traditionalist, stressing adherence to the tribal religion and cultural patterns; the moderate that retains elements of the traditional Indian heritage and customs while adjusting to the dominant white societal patterns; and the progressive, which replaces the traditional culture with the modern white beliefs and values. Educators need to be aware of these different role choices and to avoid influencing Indian students to choose a role based on the expectations of whites.

Among the cultural values basic to many tribes is an emphasis on living for today—in harmony with nature, with no time consciousness, with a concern for giving, not accumulating, a respect for age, and a desire for sharing and cooperating. These values are often in direct opposition to those stressed by the dominant culture's educational program. The white way of life is future oriented, time conscious, and competitive. It places great importance on youth, the conquest of nature, and long-term saving.

For over a century the federal government, largely through the Bureau of Indian Affairs, has assumed the responsibility for educating Native Americans to the standards of the general population. Because the Indians must live in the white man's world, their sense of survival tells them that education is the way to success, even though they may not agree with many of the practices of the schools their children attend.

Despite the availability of free schooling, only 6.2 percent of Indian females and 5.8 percent of Indian males in the Southwest have completed eight years of school. Data from the 1970 Census, however, indicated that women in the total American Indian population complete a median of 10.5 years of school with just over a third (34.6 percent) graduating from high school. Although female Indians attain more years of formal education than do males, they have been shown to be dramatically less acculturated than Indian males.

Census data also show that only 50 percent of American Indian women report English as their mother tongue. This means that English is a second language for half of the Indian women. Educational policymakers—especially at the elementary level—must be aware of the high incidence of English language deficiencies among Indian females and plan programs accordingly.

There is a real need for American Indians to participate in formulating education policy for reinforcement of the distinct tribal belief systems and value systems. Indians look upon self-determination as a necessity, especially in view of tribal diversity and the different learning styles that exist among the tribes. Yet Indian women often perceive federal programs and the women's movement as sidestepping their particular wants and strengths and threatening family unity because these programs encourage them to seek their own self-satisfying goals. This is to say that though Indians will not dispute that education is necessary for survival, they dislike the specific methods because they disrupt their culture and often have the effect of channeling Indian women into domestic jobs and other low-paying positions.

Preservation of the family with the nurturing of children within the family structure is the prime goal of Indian-made policy. Should the Indians feel a federal program to be in conflict with this policy, they can choose not to take part in it. That decision, however, is not without serious consequence: Not to participate can result in an effective block to progressive self-help by closing off economic and educational opportunities. Lack of education also prevents the American Indian from working from within the education and political systems where weighty issues must be dealt with: How, for instance, is access to educational funding on both federal and state levels gained by Indian tribes individually? Who controls and uses the funding once it is gained? How can self-determination be enacted within existing guidelines for receiving educational funding?

Thus the Indian student has two life styles to learn. On the one hand, the ways of the white, predominant culture must be learned as a survival skill, though Indian women caution against these ways being permitted to "vitiate" or influence tribal style. On the other hand, the Indian life content, which now is learned only through the home, must be learned simultaneously as standards and values. The Indian woman must be effective in both areas and aware of the appropriate responses expected of her in different situations.

Employment and job opportunities for Indian women are, naturally, affected by the level and quality of their educational background. More Indian women than any other group (86 percent) earn less than $5,000 per year. Thirty-five percent of Indian women participated in the labor force in 1970, and as a group they earned a median annual income of $1,697. Seventy percent were in the powerless and vulnerable position of clerks, operatives, and domestic service workers. Although there were two wage earners in almost half the Indian households in 1969, their median family income was a mere $3,300. American Indians, the smallest and poorest of all America's ethnic groups, "stand in a class by themselves when it comes to suffering economic deprivation," according to economist Lester Thurow.

For the most part, Indian women believe that working toward the improvement of the status of Indians as a people is where their efforts should be directed and not solely toward their status as Indian women. As a Winnebago woman put it, "We Indian women do not feel oppressed in the Indian world. We are more concerned with the problems of racial discrimination." An Isleta Pueblo woman observes that Indian women have a concept of equal rights that is different from that of the women's movement; they believe that acquiring equal rights does not necessarily mean that Indian women want to attain equal leverage in tribal matters. And Minerva White, a Seneca, recently said, "We have had women's liberation for five thousand years; we have been liberated for five thousand years, and so that is not an issue for us."

Because Indians do not make the same kinds of sex-role distinctions whites make, and because Indian women, especially those of matrilineal tribes, influence tribal economic decisions and are in decision-making positions, these women are not generally sympathetic to the women's movement. They accept the reality of social changes occurring, but ask little beyond a voice and some control over the directions of the changes that are profoundly affecting the lives within their tribe.

Asian-American Women

Asian-Americans, like American Indians, are a highly diversified ethnic group. The Asian-American population includes Koreans, Indians, Pakistanis, Vietnamese, Indonesians, Thais, Malaysians, and a wide representation of Pacific peoples such as Samoans, Guamanians, and native Hawaiians. Americans of Chinese, Japanese, and Filipino origins are also included, and because more detailed research and description are available for them, they will, for the purpose of this discussion, represent all Asian-Americans.

Asians today constitute less than 1 percent of the population in the United States, although the importance of their presence in this country, past and present, far outweighs their numbers. From a background of "unskilled" labor and objects of discrimination, Asian-Americans have reached comparatively high levels of educational and occupational achievement. Chinese and Japanese, the most prominent of the Asian-descended groups in America, are often pointed out as the "successful" minority groups.

The first Census data of 1910 showed that 78 percent of the Japanese in this country were male, as were 89 percent of the Filipinos and 90 percent of the Chinese. Because recent immigration has almost consistently introduced more females than males into each of the Asian-American communities, the sex ratios have changed considerably. The Japanese and Korean populations are now predominantly female, partly a reflection of the number of war brides brought back by returning servicemen. The Chinese and Filipinos continue to be predominantly male.

A comparison of the labor-force status of women shows that a larger percentage of Asian-American women (50 percent) work outside the home than do black (48 percent) or white women (41 percent). A little over 55 percent of Filipino women and 42 percent of Korean women work; whereas Japanese and Chinese women occupy an intermediate position with 49 percent taking jobs, according to 1970 Census data. All in all the proportion of Asian-American females gainfully employed is higher than the national average, and this does not take into account the unpaid women in family-operated businesses, since many of these women do not classify themselves as "employed."

Although many Asian-American women are highly educated, having attended or completed college, they are nevertheless concentrated in the positions of bookkeepers, secretaries, typists, file clerks, and the like. "They are qualified for better jobs," says Betty Lee Sung of the Department of Asian Studies at City College of the City University of New York, "but are the victims of sexism more than racism."

Levels of unemploymdnt of Japanese-American and Chinese-American women are generally low, even slightly lower than those for whites. In 1970, for example, the unemployment rate was only 3.7 percent for Chinese women. The problem is not in getting a job, but rather in the kind of job and the salary it pays. Many recent Chinese immigrants, fresh off the plane, can walk into one of the small garment factories scattered throughout any Chinatown or its peripheral area and start working the next day. They work by the piece and their hours are fairly flexible. Piece work at low rates is always available.

The presence of very young children has not limited the level of occupational achievement for young working Asian women. Chinese mothers show higher levels of occupational achievement than childless, never-married Chinese women. This is true also for Filipino women, although to a lesser extent than for the Chinese. This situation may represent a cultural carry-over from the traditional Asian pattern in which middle class Asian mothers are inclined to be employed. By Asian custom, older children help to take care of younger ones, thereby relieving mothers of these family duties during the day. Hence, the Asian "day-care" program is conducted within the home and family.

Chinese-American women are marrying later and limiting their families probably because they are spending more years in school. In 1970, the median years of schooling for each Asian-American group was slightly above the white attainment of 12.1 years. Today, differences in years of completed schooling among Asians and whites of both sexes have virtually disappeared.

Census data for 1970 indicate that 23 percent of Filipino and 58 percent of Chinese-American women between 18 and 24 years of age are in college. About three-fourths of all Japanese-Americans finish high school. Figures like these indicate that many families have shed the centuries-old belief that females are spoiled for wifehood and motherhood if they acquire some education. It is generally the foreign-born female who is the most deprived and, hence, the most handicapped. Her occupational sphere is, therefore, extremely circumscribed and limited to the most simple and menial jobs.

Many Americans are unaware that more Chinese-Americans are born abroad than are born in the United States. The foreign-born ratio will probably become greater as immigration exceeds native births. In essence, the Chinese-American population is largely a first-generation or immigrant-generation population. The tremendous adjustment that first-generation Chinese-Americans must make puts them at a disadvantage in every respect. They must re-educate themselves completely and quickly.

Most Americans assume that Asian-Americans have no social problems, an assumption which restricts the access of Asian-Americans to funds available to minority groups. As a result they have been forced to form self-help organizations in their own communities, an action leading to the misconception that Asians "take care of their own."

One segment of the Asian population most in need of help are those who cannot speak, read, or write English. Illiteracy is generally a problem with those over 45, especially the women. The younger generations are highly educated and bilingual, regardless of sex. However, in the 1970 Census, only four percent of the Chinese living in New York listed English as their mother tongue. In California, 12 percent and in Hawaii, 44 percent did so. That the Chinese have clung to their language more tenaciously than most other national groups is commendable and could provide a national resource of bilingual people.

Another problem Asian-Americans often encounter is the American cultural values that are in conflict with many traditional Asian values. For example, many Asian cultures have emphasized strict loyalty to the family, which trains children to avoid controversial, potentially embarrassing situations. Strict self-control and discipline were mandatory. As a result, Asians, especially women, often have appeared to be reserved, self-conscious, and reticent, finding continuity, permanence, and personal security in the close relations of the family. In contrast, dominant American culture now comprises a majority of single, nuclear families with few multigenerational living arrangements.

Another example would be American competitiveness based on "each for himself," a notion alien to most Asians. However, in the process of acculturation and upward mobility, many Asians have adopted the more expressive and assertive style of the dominant culture. Betty Lee Sung asserts that the tendency is becoming increasingly prevalent for Asian-Americans to believe that, in order to adjust to living in the United States, one must embrace the American way in toto and cast off the Asian heritage completely. She also believes that great psychological damage will result for these Asian-Americans. Instead, she holds, Asian-American women and men should strive for a culturally pluralistic society in which they can preserve their heritages while contributing to American social, civic, and educational life.

Like many foreign women, Asian-American women have been neatly categorized by stereotype milled in white imaginations. Asian women are often described as being docile, submissive, and sexless; or exotic, sexy, and diabolical. They are often presented as objects or commodities rather than as persons with ideas, aspirations, talents, and feelings.

A situation familiar to many Asian women comes as a consequence of recent immigration. Since the end of World War II, more than 500,000 women of foreign nationality have entered the United States as spouses of Americans. Over one-third of these women were from Asian countries. Professor Bok-Lim Kim of the University of Illinois has found that many of these women experience a host of adjustment problems. Reports of severe physical abuse and deprivation are not uncommon. In one study made at Washington State, Professor Kim noted that divorce or separation among Asian wives of military men resulted in over 20 percent of those in the study becoming female heads of households. (This figure is in contrast to the 6 percent of Chinese-American and 8 percent of Filipino-American female heads of households.) These Asian wives are often unable to seek help because of their isolation, lack of proficiency in English, unfamiliarity with the life style, and fear of outside contacts.

Young Asian-American women, especially those who are third generation, are feeling a void and are expressing a need and desire to rediscover their ethnicity. These women are more liberated and more assertive. They are challenging the monocultural ideal of the majority society to acknowledge, analyze, and incorporate Asian-American women and men at all social, political, educational, and economical levels. Fundamental changes in the American educational process toward a goal of cultural pluralism is a realistic response to their peculiar needs and strengths.

Minority women by and large are concerned with how Anglo society—its educational institutions in particular—has attempted to divorce them from their cultural heritage and alienate them from their men. They want to share the belief that the only route to fulfillment of the American Dream is by perseverance and education. Yet the present educational system often militates against such goals for minorities and especially females.

Many minority women are high school dropouts. Consequently they look to secondary school programs to be made more relevant and available to them. In like vein higher education, a recent alternative for many minority women, needs to be demystified. College role models in their immediate families are still rarely found because most minority women in college today are the first in their families to be there. Setting this kind of precedent puts pressure on the young women, brought on by expectations from both their families and themselves. Those who make it through four years of college soon become painfully aware that the job benefits which should follow are often limited. Many college-educated minority women are unable to get white-collar jobs at a professional level.

The fact is that minority women frequently explain their problems in economic terms. The kinds of jobs open to them is a smarting issue to these women. Of 36 million women in the labor force, 4.7 million are minorities, constituting more than 40 percent of all minority workers. Discriminatory hiring practices based on racist and sexist factors still prevail and are just further complicated when minority women have educational attainments, the more educated often finding themselves underemployed and underpaid. It is often the case that both white and minority women with some college education earn less than minority men with less than a high school education.

Generally, however, the more education a woman has the more likely she is to be in the skilled or professional labor force. New job opportunities in expanding occupations and additional schooling are almost certain to place more minority women in the labor force.

Statistics indicate that most minority women workers are high school graduates. March 1974 figures showed 61 percent had graduated from high school, including 10 percent who had completed four or more years of college. The comparable figures for white women were 75 and 14 percent, respectively. Because minority women complete a median 12.3 years of schooling, the educational system must plan and implement instruction that will meet their special needs during these 12 years.

One purpose of the educational system is to equip all learners with satisfying and rewarding competencies for entering the world of work in the field of one's choice. The curriculum and instruction used in preparing the professionals who will work with minority girls and women must reflect the heritage, needs, and concerns of the various minorities. Cultural pluralism, a relatively new idea in education, addresses the cultural differences of minority women and informs majority men and women about this diversity. This pluralistic concept is the hope that ethnic women have in getting others to understand, promote, and respect differences in cultural patterns and learning styles that are so widespread in America—and, not incidentally, in advancing themselves in the dominant culture.

POSSIBLE STRATEGIES TO MEET THE EDUCATIONAL NEEDS AND STRENGTHS OF MINORITY WOMEN

Federal education agencies and foundations
- Conduct and encourage research into the problems and concerns shared by minority women in the area of education.
- Organize on national or regional levels a clearinghouse for information exchange on minority women and relevant resource personnel, materials, and programs.

State departments of education
- Interpret Title IX with a sensitivity to multiculturism, recognizing the double jeopardy of sex and race.

- Include multicultural female representatives in planning and developing programs for minority women and girls.
- Encourage and provide equal employment opportunities for hiring minority women in administrative and decision-making positions.
- Retrain educators, counselors, and administrators to sensitize them to the special needs and concerns of minority female students.
- Require teacher training and certification programs to include intense self-evaluation sensitivity to multiculturism.

Local education agencies
- Include minority women and community members on the board of directors or trustees.
- Encourage minority women to prepare for career advancement and provide adequate training opportunities.

Education institutions (preschool through college)
- Recruit minority women into administrative, faculty, and student ranks.
- Provide special stipends and allowances for minority female students from low-income families.
- Adopt day care, tutorial, and counseling services to enable minority women to partake of educational opportunities.
- Initiate special placement efforts for minority female graduates.
- Expand and enrich adult education opportunities so that parents and children are exposed to acculturation at a more closely related pace.
- Encourage and preserve bilingualism.
- Emphasize in school and college curriculums the literature, music, art, dance, games, and sports of minority cultures.
- Make effective use of community resources and develop incentives for community participation.
- Evaluate regularly and systematically school programs that involve minorities.

Being a Man: Background for Teachers

(From *Being a Man—A Unit of Instructional Activities on Male Role Stereotyping*, U.S. Department of Health, Education, and Welfare, Office of Education, 1977, David Sadker)

Defining the Male Role Stereotype

From cradle to grave, the pressures of sex role stereotyping serve to channel and limit male and female behavior. There is, for example, no genetic reason why male infants should be dressed in blue and female infants in pink. The only apparent purpose for such a practice is to aid adults who might unwittingly compliment a male infant's "long lashes" or a female infant's "husky build." The colors serve to signal adults as to the appropriate behavior. Pink elicits "Isn't she sweet!" (Sweet may be replaced by "adorable," "beautiful," "cunning," "a knockout," etc.) Such comments may be complemented by soft touches and warm hugs. Blue, on the other hand, elicits "husky fellow," "looks like a football player," and "tough guy." The accompanying physical treatment given to boys is less warm than that given to girls, and, in fact, one study revealed that after six months of age, boys are picked up and hugged less often than girls are.[1]

As male infants become young boys, the differential treatment intensifies, and the lessons on male role expectations become more frequent. A boy who rejects aspects of this role is reprimanded more severely, in fact, than is his female counterpart. A girl who does not follow the socially approved expectations for females is often described as "going through a phase." She is allowed to be a "tomboy"—at least for a period of time. However, a boy who rejects the male role stereotype is awarded no such tolerance. The term "janeboy" does not exist.

Both at home and in school, boys are made to conform to rigid sex role expectations. Even the newspapers provide no relief. A popular "advice to the reader" column recently featured a letter from a parent who was deeply concerned because her young son was playing with dolls. There was no acknowledgment that doll play can be a harmless and, in fact, valuable way for boys to rehearse future parental roles. The columnist advised that if the "problem" continued, the boy might be "sick," and recommended that the child receive professional help.

Wherever boys turn, this sex role socialization continues. On television and in films, they view thousands of hours of violence and tough masculine models. From parents and counselors, most boys are channeled into male-oriented occupations and are encouraged to fulfill a masculine value system. To peers they must prove their toughness. So pervasive is the pressure that few boys are ever permitted to seriously question the worth and appropriateness of the male role stereotype. Before we explore the limitations of the masculine mystique, we must take a closer look at what this stereotype entails. As we examine the lessons of the male stereotype, however, it is important to remember that the behaviors described can be positive and healthy qualities when displayed by either males or females in situations where these behaviors are appropriate. They become negative and limiting, however, when they are required for or permitted to only one sex and when they are applied to *all* situations. The qualities discussed below in "The Lessons of the Male Stereotype" are described in their most extreme and stereotyped form, because this is often the way that they impact on young (and not-so-young) males.

The Lessons of the Male Stereotype

Lesson One—Stifle It

"Crybaby" may represent a common childhood taunt, but its echoes follow young boys into manhood. It is "unmanly" to cry. Boys are supposed to be strong and unemotional.

By five or six years of age, boys know that they are supposed to show neither fear nor tears.[2] As men, they have learned to present a strong and unemotional facade. The "strong, silent" type has become the model. Small disappointments and major catastrophes are to be treated with the same stoic response. Concealing fear, sorrow, doubt, and tenderness is a mark of being a "real man."

Lesson Two—Choose Your Occupation (from the following list only!)

Although our society offers a wide variety of potential careers, sex typing restricts the choices of boys and girls. For girls, the restrictions have traditionally been very severe, limiting females to relatively few socially acceptable careers which are often extensions of the nurturing role. Boys also encounter career restrictions. Boys who consider becoming teachers of very young children, nurses, dancers, or secretaries absorb social criticism for their occupational choice—or change their decisions.

Lesson Three—Money Makes the Man

Although acceptable career options for men are socially restricted, at least one characteristic of any acceptable occupation remains constant: It must pay well. The male has been designated as the primary, and often only, financial provider for the family. In fact, a man's ability to earn a substantial income has become a measure not only of his success, but of his masculinity as well. The size of a man's paycheck is a measure of his worth. A woman may glow in the green radiance emanating from her husband's wallet, pleased and proud to have pulled off a "real catch." To males, the lesson is all too clear: In order to be successful and desirable, earn, earn, earn.

Lesson Four—Winning at Any Cost

From the early years on, boys are taught the lessons of intense competition. On the athletic field, in school, and even in their social lives, most boys are driven to compete and to win, no matter what the cost. As adults, this cult of competition continues as many men vie to get ahead of one another for the best paying jobs and the earliest promotions.

The athletic field provides numerous examples of this pervasive competitive ethic. Uncontrollable anger from an eight-year-old second baseman on a losing Little League team is evidence of the early inculcation of this competitive drive. Former football coach Vince Lombardi summed it up well when he said, "Winning is not the most important thing. It's the only thing."

Lesson Five—Acting Tough

With few frontiers left to conquer and few wild animals left to subdue, men are taught nevertheless to be strong and tough. In our technological society, this toughness has become redirected at dominating women, conquering other men, and questing for power and money. Acting tough includes not only hiding emotions and competing at all costs but also childishly demonstrating personal strength. It involves the ability to dish it out and to "take it," even when refusal to capitulate or compromise involves severe physical and psychological loss. Reason and compassion are frequently the victims when a man demonstrates his virility by acting tough.

Acting tough is required in both personal and public behavior; it is clearly valued in many of our most prestigious social roles, from corporate executive to military officer.

The Male Machine[3]

Marc Feigen Fasteau has summed up this masculine stereotype by way of analogy: As men learn these lessons in masculinity, they assume machinelike qualities. The complete fulfillment of the male stereotype results in a functional, efficient machine. Such a man/machine seizes the offensive and tackles jobs with a fervor. Personal issues wait along a sidetrack as he rumbles on straight ahead to the victory he needs. Victory reinforces his competitive drive. Defeat is marked without emotion, and serves only to strengthen his resolve. His gears run efficiently, if not effortlessly, and his relationship to other male machines is one of respect, never intimacy. The male machine is programed to operate in certain acceptable areas, and tends to become dysfunctional if forced into "inappropriate" occupations, like nursing or secretarial work. The machine is geared for victory, and victory is demonstrated by success, power, and, of course, money.

Men who buy into this image and who adopt the masculine stereotype are doing so at great cost. For inside the male machine lives a human being, an individual with the potential to go beyond this mechanical existence and to live a fuller, more diverse, complete, and longer life. But living in a society that molds and rewards the male machine makes it difficult to perceive the cost of male sex role stereotyping. The next section briefly reviews some of these costs.

The Cost of the Male Role Stereotype

Hidden costs have become a way of life in our society. The new washing machine, advertised for $199, costs $257 after installation, tax, delivery, and the $10 charge for "harvest gold" are added on. Hidden costs.

Male sex role stereotyping results in one of the great hidden costs of our society. This cost frequently goes undetected, for it is a natural part of the American landscape. But the cost is real and devastating.

Cost 1—Early Problems

Boys are pressured early to meet the demands of the sex role stereotype. Parents generally encourage their children to develop interests in those areas that they consider appropriate for their sex and discourage their children—particularly their sons—from activities that they consider appropriate for the opposite sex.[4] Such shaping of sex-typed behaviors may have consequences for the school performance of young males. Numerous studies have documented that in our culture young males experience a significantly higher frequency of reading difficulties than do young females. This is not the case, however, in cultures in which reading is typed as an important component of the male role.[5]

Cost 2—Barriers Between Men

Men who are committed to the traditional masculine stereotype find little time or reason to establish close relationships with other men. The competitive drive makes them adversaries, and reduces the desire for cooperation and friendship. The inability to share emotions and feelings hinders honest personal communication. To protect the image of self-reliant toughness, and to hide potential vulnerabilities, the stereotyped male develops an invisible communication barrier that keeps other men at a distance. The traditional male image is preserved, but at a high cost—nothing less than the friendship of other human beings.

Cost 3—Barriers Between Men and Women

Many aspects of the male stereotype inhibit positive relationships between men and women. The overemphasized male commitment to a career can detract from the quantity and quality of time men spend with

74

women. The inability of some men to share their feelings and self-doubts—in some cases the inability of men to be in touch with their personal feelings—may detract from an honest and open relationship. The pressure felt by men to continually compete and succeed, the same pressure which alienates them from their fellow men, also may restrict and limit the quality of their relationship with women.

In marriage, the male stereotype continues to limit the quality of male-female relationships. This is especially true because of the increasing number of wives now exploring careers outside the home. These women do not seek a marital partner who will play the dominant role of sole economic provider and family breadwinner. Rather, they seek partners willing and able to share in the family's economic venture. Men enmeshed in the male stereotype perceive the notion of a wife at work as threatening, perhaps even an indication of the husband's inability as family provider. This marital stress increases when working wives expect their husbands to depart even further from the male stereotype and share in the household chores. Men who perceive these chores as "women's work" and "unmanly" create further marital tension. Many of today's women are openly demanding a sharing of their traditional homemaking roles, and a husband unable to grow beyond the male stereotype may find his marriage just another statistic in the mushrooming divorce rate.

Cost 4—Weekend Fathers

The fulfillment of role demands pulls many men away not only from their wives, but from their children as well. Long hours invested in career building and moneymaking are at the expense of time spent with children. One recent study revealed that a majority of new fathers had never changed a diaper[6]—an interesting comment on the lack of contact between father and child. For many of these fathers, this estranged relationship continues as their children grow into adolescence. Mothers often assume the major parenting function, as men become weekend fathers. The distance between children and their fathers is another measure of the cost of sex role stereotyping.

Cost 5—The Career "Lock-in"

Because of the pressure to earn, earn, earn, men often find themselves victims of the career lock-in. Initially they are forced to consider only the more lucrative positions, even if they are not interested in these jobs. Once involved in their chosen careers, there is no exit. If, after 10 or 20 years, a man becomes bored or uninterested in his work, he literally cannot afford to explore alternatives. With the family's financial well-being totally in his hands, his decisions are no longer his own. Sex role stereotyping locks women into household tasks, and men into a job that brings money, but not necessarily self-fulfillment.

Cost 6—The Leisure and Retirement "Lockout"

The other side of the career lock-in is the leisure and retirement lockout. When men devote a great deal of time first to competing for the best jobs and promotions and then to guarding and maintaining their hard-won positions, there is little time left to develop leisure interests. The single-track nature of many men's lives becomes even more apparent during the retirement years. At a time when the rewards of lifelong efforts should be reaped, these men find themselves drifting aimlessly as their well-trodden paths to the office or business door are closed off. Without work, they are also without direction or purpose. The suicide rate for retired men is several times that of retired women.[7]

Cost 7—Physical Disability and Death

The obvious muscular superiority of most men over most women leads to a common misconception: that men are stronger than women. Since we live in a world where muscular strength is of less and less importance, endurance and other areas of physical strength become more crucial. And in those areas, men are the weaker sex. They have a greater susceptibility to stress. After years of driving to compete, striving to get ahead, shouldering economic burdens, and hiding their doubts and fears from others, men fall victim to heart attack and stroke. Men are likely to die at an earlier age than women: the average lifespan for women exceeds that of men by about eight years. Although the susceptibility of men to serious disease and earlier death may be due in part to biological differences, the economic and psychological burdens of male sex role demands may take a significant toll in the physical well-being of men.[8]

Cost 8—Society's Masculine Nature

The preponderance of men in the leadership positions of our institutions casts a long shadow over the very nature of our society. The tough, competitive, emotionless, male role stereotype permeates our political, economic, and military institutions. The aggression of corporate executives "on the move," the "flexing of muscles" and the "rattling of swords" of political leaders, and the stoic masculinity of military men all reflect the male sex role stereotype on a grand scale. At these institutional levels, the effects of male stereotyping touch the lives of all society's children.

Many of the same costs inflicted on men individually are also inflicted on the society at large. The single-minded commitment to "winning" permeated our institutions, sometimes leading to illegal and immoral acts in order to win a profitable contract or to pass laws in the self-interest of legislators. Conscience and reflection are submerged as private and public institutions become involved in a headlong and sometimes mindless mission of self-interest. Lack of emotionality is considered a societal virtue and given the respectable label of "efficiency."

In international affairs, many nations have adopted the masculine mystique as part of their foreign policy. A "show of strength," a lust to protect or add to a nation's territory, the aggression of and competition between nations—all this and more reflects aspects of machismo, the masculine stereotype, on an international scale.

It is impossible to predict how different the world might be if cooperation, compassion, and interpersonal honesty were the hallmarks of international relations. And unfortunately, we do live in a world in which the resort to force may be necessary in issues concerning national self-defense and human freedom. But frequently, nations are too eager to prove their strength through tough words and tough actions. And the world is a less safe, less sane place because of it.

Confronting the Male Role Stereotype

It is time that we understand and confront the damaging effects of our society's traditional conceptions of sex roles. As teachers, we can participate in moving the next generation beyond these limiting definitions of masculinity and femininity. Boys and girls are not polar extremes, in spite of all the lessons of the socialization process. Society should accept boys who are dependent and gentle as well as girls who are strong and assertive. It is time society recognized the universal and fundamental human qualities of all its children.

The human potential lost to society as a result of sex role stereotyping is impossible to estimate. Psychological studies suggest that females who adopt the feminine stereotype score low on self-esteem and self-acceptance, but high on anxiety, relative to females who do not adopt the stereotype. Men who accept the male stereotype also demonstrate high anxiety and low self-acceptance relative to other males. Both males and females who are highly sex stereotyped score lower on creativity and intelligence tests than those who are not as sex stereotyped.[9]

In the final analysis, when all the psychological and sociological costs are tallied, when all the philosophical and legal arguments for equality are advanced, the real human commitment to liberation for men and women remains an intensely personal one. In the next few years, if society is to alleviate the restrictions of male stereotyping, it will be as a result of the beliefs and actions of individuals. The willingness and ability of individual teachers, men and women, to confront this issue, can be a significant force in moving our society away from the debilitating effects of sexism.

Title IX of the Education Amendments, 1972

(Reprinted from *A Guide to Federal Laws and Regulations Prohibiting Sex Discrimination,* Clearinghouse Publication No. 46, U.S. Commission on Civil Rights, July 1976, revised.)

Most educational institutions across the United States receive federal financial assistance; these include preschool programs, elementary and secondary school systems, four-year colleges and universities, vocational and technical schools, two-year community and junior colleges, and graduate and professional schools. Title IX of the Education Amendments of 1972[1] and HEW's Title IX regulations[2] prohibit educational institutions which receive federal funds from discriminating on the basis of sex.

Coverage

This prohibition covers educational programs, employment, health benefits, housing, athletics, admissions, and financial aid, and all other programs and services of the institution, except fraternities and sororities.[3] Military schools and schools operated by religious organizations whose tenets are inconsistent with the provisions of Title IX, are exempt from coverage.

Vocational, professional, graduate, and public undergraduate schools may not discriminate on the basis of sex in admissions, but private undergraduate schools, schools which have traditionally admitted only individuals of one sex, and public and private preschools, elementary and secondary schools (except where such schools are vocational) are exempt from the provisions with regard to admissions only. Schools which are in transition from single-sex to co-educational institutions are allowed seven years to complete the process, during which they may continue to make admissions decisions on the basis of sex.

Examples of discrimination forbidden by these amendments include: refusal of a board of education to hire or promote qualified women as principals in the school system, refusal of a college to provide housing of comparable quality and cost to students of both sexes, or maintenance of sex-segregated classes in business, vocational, technical, home economics, music, and adult education courses or programs.

What Is Required

An education program or activity receiving federal funds must afford employees, students, and potential employees and students equal employment opportunity and equal opportunity to participate in and receive the benefits of all educational programs and activities, without regard to sex.

Specific obligations include the following:

All educational institutions are required to refrain from sex discrimination (except as otherwise noted). Where the director of HEW's Office for Civil Rights finds that an institution has discriminated on the basis of sex in an education program or activity, the institution must take remedial action to overcome the effects of such discrimination. However, in the absence of a determination of prior acts of discrimination based on sex, the institution is not required to act affirmatively to overcome limited participation by persons of a particular sex, although it may choose to do so.

Generally, institutions may not utilize tests, counseling, or recruiting methods which have a disproportionately adverse effect on persons on the basis of sex, either for admission to programs or activities or for employment. In admissions, testing or counseling materials may be different for males and females if they cover the same interest areas and occupations and the use of such different materials is shown to be essential to eliminate sex bias. In employment, testing may be different for males and females if it is shown to be valid in predicting successful performance and if alternatives are unavailable. Recruitment of members of one sex may be used remedially to overcome the effects of past discrimination, but may not otherwise be used if it has a discriminatory effect.

Institutions may not make pre-admission or pre-employment inquires about actual or potential marital, parental, or family status of individuals. For both students and employees, childbirth, pregnancy, termination of pregnancy and recovery therefrom must be treated as any other temporary disability. In the absence of a leave policy, the institution must treat these factors as a justification for a leave of absence without pay for a reasonable period of time, at the conclusion of which the employee must be reinstated in a comparable position without a decrease in pay, privileges, and/or promotional opportunities. Students must be reinstated at their previous status and may not be discriminated against or excluded from a program or activity unless they voluntarily request to participate in a separate program or activity.

If the institution participates in the administration of scholarships, awards, or fellowships which discriminate on the basis of sex, it must provide reasonable opportunities for similar awards for members of the other sex. In the case of athletics, the institution must provide reasonable opportunities for scholarship awards for members of each sex in proportion to the number of students of each sex participating in interscholastic or intercollegiate athletics.

Institutions may provide separate housing based on sex, but may not impose different rules, fees, or requirements or provide different benefits to one sex. Housing for women and men must be comparable in quality and cost and proportionate in quantity to the number of students of each sex applying for it.

Institutions may provide separate toilet, locker room, and shower facilities on the basis of sex, but the facilities provided for students of one sex must be comparable to those provided for students of the other sex.

The use of particular textbooks and other curricular materials are not prohibited by Title IX, regardless of content. However, courses, programs, and activities may not be segregated by sex except in the case of choruses with vocal range requirements resulting in a single sex chorus, courses on human sexuality on the elementary and secondary level, and body contact sports. Physical education programs on the elementary level must be integrated by July 21, 1976, and by July 21, 1978, above the elementary level.

Separate athletic teams may be maintained for sports involving competitive skills and body contact. For non-contact sports only, if no separate team for a particular sport exists for one sex and previous opportunities were limited for that sex to participate, all persons must be permitted to try out for the existing team. Teams for contact sports may remain single-sex, even if no team is available for the excluded sex. Institutions are permitted to make unequal aggregate and per capita expenditures for members of each sex on a team or for separate male and female teams so long as this does not interfere with equality of opportunity for members of each sex. Necessary funds must be provided for teams for each sex.

Complaints

Each institution must adopt and publish complaint procedures and designate at least one employee to carry out its Title IX responsibilities, including investigation of complaints. The institution must notify all students and employees of the appointed employee's name, office address, and telephone number.

In addition, a complaint may be filed with the Office for Civil Rights of the Department of Health, Education, and Welfare by any person (or a representative) who believes herself or himself or either sex as a class to be subjected to discrimination prohibited by Title IX. The written complaint should be filed with:

Director, Office for Civil Rights
Department of Health, Education, and Welfare
330 Independence Ave., S.W.
Washington, D.C. 20201

Complaints must be filed within 180 days of the alleged discrimination, but HEW may extend this deadline.

HEW may investigate where a complaint has been made or where there are other indications that the educational institution is discriminating on the basis of sex. HEW will informally attempt to bring the institution into compliance with the requirements of Title IX. Once a complaint has been filed, the complainant is no longer involved, and it is the responsibility of HEW to resolve it.

Enforcement and Sanctions

In addition to investigations initiated by a complaint, HEW may conduct periodic compliance reviews. Where an educational institution is found to be discriminating on the basis of sex and HEW finds that this cannot be corrected informally, it may terminate or refuse to grant funds to the institution. Before such action may be taken, HEW must allow an opportunity for a hearing and must find that there will not be voluntary compliance with the nondiscrimination requirements. In addition, HEW may refer the matter to the Attorney General of the United States with a recommendation that legal action be taken, or take any other action authorized by law.

Title IX and Grievance Procedures

(Reprinted from *Title IX Grievance Procedures: An Introductory Manual,* U.S. Department of Health, Education, and Welfare, Office of Education, Martha Matthews and Shirley McCune.)

Title IX of the Education Amendments of 1972 requires that:

> No person in the United States shall, on the basis of sex, be excluded from participation in, be denied the benefits of, or be subjected to discrimination under any education program or activity receiving federal financial assistance.

The regulation to implement Title IX, issued by the Office for Civil Rights, Department of Health, Education, and Welfare (OCR/HEW), became effective on July 21, 1975. It specifies detailed prohibitions of sex discrimination in education agencies and institutions receiving federal funds. Sex discrimination is prohibited in:

- Admissions to most schools
- Treatment of students, including:
  —access to programs and courses
  —access to and use of school facilities
  —counseling and guidance materials, tests, and practices
  —vocational education
  —physical education
  —competitive athletics
  —graduation requirements
  —student rules, regulations, and benefits
  —the treatment of married and/or pregnant students
  —housing
  —financial assistance
  —health services
  —school-sponsored extracurricular activities
  —most other aid, benefits, or services
- Employment
  —access to employment, including:
    - recruitment policies and practices
    - advertising
    - application procedures
    - testing and interviewing practices

—hiring and promotion, including:
  - selection practices
  - application of nepotism policies
  - demotion, lay off, termination
  - tenure
—compensation, including:
  - wages and salaries
  - extra compensations
—job assignments, including:
  - classification and position descriptions
  - lines of progression
  - seniority lists
  - assignment and placement
—leaves of absence, including:
  - leaves for temporary disability
  - childbearing leave and related medical conditions
  - childrearing leave
—fringe benefits, including:
  - insurance plans
  - retirement plans
  - vacation time
  - travel opportunities
  - selection and support for training
  - employer-sponsored programs
—labor organization contracts or professional agreements

The regulation also provides that complaints alleging Title IX violations by a recipient agency or institution may be filed with the Office for Civil Rights, HEW. OCR has the authority to investigate complaints, or to review compliance in the absence of complaints. If violations are found, OCR may attempt to achieve compliance through conciliation, institute administrative proceedings to terminate federal funds, or refer the case to the Department of Justice for court action to effect compliance without termination, withholding, or denial of eligibility for federal funds.

One of the unique aspects of the Title IX regulation is its delineation of procedures which education agencies and institutions receiving federal funds are required to implement in order to ensure and monitor compliance with Title IX requirements for nondiscrimination. Two of these required procedures—one for the designation of an employee responsible for the coordination of agency or institutional efforts to comply with Title IX, the other for the adoption and publication of an internal grievance procedure for the resolution of complaints[1] under Title IX—place responsibility on the agency or institution for the establishment and maintenance of a mechanism whereby students and employees may seek an end to and redress from illegal sex discrimination and whereby the agency or institution may continually be apprised of and evaluate possible discriminatory policies and practices and develop its own strategies or programs for the correction of discrimination.

These two provisions of the Title IX regulation read as follows:

§86.8 Designation of responsible employee and adoption of grievance procedures.
(a) Designation of responsible employee. Each recipient shall designate at least one employee to coordinate its efforts to comply with and carry out its responsibilities under this . . . [regulation], including any investigation of any complaint communicated to such recipient alleging any actions which would be prohibited by this . . . [regulation]. The recipient shall notify all its students and employees of the name, office, address, and telephone number of the employee or the employees appointed pursuant to this paragraph.
(b) Complaint procedure of recipient. A recipient shall adopt and publish grievance procedures providing for prompt and equitable resolution of student and employee complaints alleging any action which would be prohibited by this . . . [regulation].

All recipient agencies and institutions were required to comply with these requirements by July 21, 1976.

With its issuance of the regulation to implement Title IX, the Department of Health, Education, and Welfare indicated that the primary intent of these two provisions is to "facilitate compliance and prompt correction of complaints without resort to federal involvement." The existence of an agency or institutional grievance procedure does not affect the right of an individual or group to file a federal complaint regarding possible Title IX violations with the Office for Civil Rights, HEW, without utilizing the internal procedure of the agency or institution, simultaneously with the filing of an internal grievance, or after the unsatisfactory resolution of a grievance under the agency/institutional procedure. A usable and effective agency or institutional procedure can, however, minimize the complainant's need for recourse to the federal process, and offer both the complainant and the agency or institution the prospect of an expeditious resolution of issues and the development of compliance activities which are best suited to the particular situation involved.

In order to facilitate the implementation of a grievance procedure which can most effectively meet the needs of an individual education agency or institution and its students and employees, the Title IX regulation does not specify a structure for the grievance procedure. It requires only that the procedure provide for the "prompt and equitable resolution of student and employee complaints."

Note: For detailed and comprehensive information in this area, we suggest Title IX Grievance Procedures: An Introductionary Manual, *available from the Superintendent of Documents, U.S. Government Printing Office, Washington, D.C. 20402. Price $2.50, Stock No. 017-080-01711-3.*

Title IX Action Plan

(The following is excerpted from the "Title IX Action Plan," as approved by the Board of Education, the Montgomery County—Maryland—Public Schools on June 27, 1977.)

Section of Regulation and Recommendation

86.8 Designation of Responsible Employee and Adoption of Grievance Procedure
   1. Each school and office should designate a liason person to deal with Title IX compliance on the local level.
   2. Designated individuals should receive workshop training on Title IX, issues of sex role stereotyping, and information regarding remediation resulting from the institutional self-evaluation.
   3. Grievance procedures should be reviewed on a biennial basis to determine that specified Title IX regulations have been included.

86.31 Educational Programs and Activities
   1. Schools should eliminate any existing restrictions in extracurricular programs based on sex.
   2. Countywide student government organizations should be briefed on Title IX.

86.34 Access to Courses:
   Physical Education
   1. In-service programs should be provided for all secondary physical education teachers. The in-service should include information on Title IX as well as additional training on working with coeducational programs.

86.34 Access to Courses:
   General
   1. Montgomery County Public Schools should utilize affirmative action to encourage female enrollment in advanced mathematics, chemistry, and physics; and develop a plan to accomplish this task.
   2. Mandated Montgomery County Public Schools Tests should be reported and evaluated by sex in order to determine if differences in achievement by males and females are evident and if remedial action needs to be taken.
   3. Assessment should be made of courses having 80 percent or more

single sex enrollment to determine that this enrollment is not because of policies or practices of Montgomery County Public Schools or employees.

86.36 Counseling and Use of Appraisal and Counseling Materials

1. Training programs should be developed for counselors on Title IX and sex-role stereotyping. These programs would aid in assuring the local schools' compliance with Title IX in the course enrollment area.
2. The occupational outlook section of the Department of Labor should be asked to conduct workshops for counselors, vocational and career personnel regarding work-life expectancy predictions for women/men and job outlook for the workforce 1985-1990.
3. There should be a reaffirmation/review of the policy that students may see the counselor of their choice.
4. Career education programs at schools which use citizen/parent participants should be carefully screened for sex and occupational balance.
5. Career education programs and materials should be given publicity in school publications.
6. Efforts should continue to be taken to provide students in elementary schools with non-stereotyped concepts of careers and roles.

86.41 Athletics

1. There should be a purposeful educational program developed at all schools regarding possibilities of participation and competition in intramural, junior varsity, and varsity athletics.
2. Students on both the junior and senior high level should be surveyed with a carefully constructed questionnaire to determine:
   a. Interest level for intramural, junior varsity, and varsity sports.
   b. Obstructions to participation in such program.
   c. Current programs that should be continued as well as needed additions or alternations.
3. A student, staff, citizen advisory committee should be developed to oversee the compliance of Montgomery County Public Schools with Title IX within the given time frame as outlined by the law.
4. An evaluation of scheduling for male/female competitive athletic events should be completed to ascertain:
   a. Opportunity for public to be in attendance
   b. Opportunity for parents/family to be in attendance
   c. Opportunity to become revenue producing
   d. Opportunity to attend all classes in the regular school day.

Staff

1. The position of Title IX Coordinator should be a fulltime equivalent position.
2. In order to increase the level of awareness of all staff, the *Bulletin* should periodically contain an article that discusses the resources

available to help staff members to develop non-sexist instructional programs.

3. All candidates for administrative and supervisory positions should be queried regarding their understanding of the Title IX regulations.

4. Ongoing contact should be maintained with publications and agencies that deal with providing greater career opportunities for women at policy-making levels.

Committee

Community, staff, and student involvement is imperative to assure compliance with Title IX and the proper implementation of future remediation as outlined in this report. It is recommended that an ongoing advisory committee be established by the superintendent of schools.

Guide for Evaluating Sex Stereotyping in Reading Materials

Developed by the Committee on Sexism and Reading of the International Reading Association

Directions: Place a check in the appropriate space. Most items should be evaluated for each sex.

	Almost always	Occa-sionally	Rarely
1. Are girls and boys, men and women consistently represented in equal balance?	___	___	___
2. Do boys and girls participate equally in both physical and intellectual activities?	___	___	___
3. Do girls and boys each receive positive recognition for their endeavors? Females	___	___	___
Males	___	___	___
4. Do boys and girls, fathers and mothers participate in a wide variety of domestic chores, not only the ones traditional for their sex? Females	___	___	___
Males	___	___	___
5. Do both girls and boys have a variety of choices and are they encouraged to aspire to various goals, including nontraditional ones if they show such inclination? Females	___	___	___
Males	___	___	___
6. Are both boys and girls shown developing independent lives, independently meeting challenges and finding their own solutions? Females	___	___	___
Males	___	___	___
7. Are women and men shown in a variety of occupations, including nontraditional ones? When women are portrayed as fulltime homemakers, are they depicted as competent and decisive? Females	___	___	___
Males	___	___	___
8. Do characters deprecate themselves because of their sex? (Example: "I'm only a girl.") Do others use denigrating language in this regard? (Example: "That's just like a woman.") Females	___	___	___
Males	___	___	___

9. Do the illustrations stereotype the characters, either in accordance to the dictates of the text or in contradiction to it?

Females ___ ___ ___
Males ___ ___ ___

10. Is inclusionary language used? (For example, "police officer" instead of "policeman," "staffed by" instead of "manned by," "all students will submit the assignment" instead of "each student will submit his assignment," and so on.

___ ___ ___

The Why of a Workshop

By Mary Ellen Verheyden-Hilliard

A workshop on sex equality in education provides a place where counselors, teachers, and administrators can begin to understand the serious long-range results of sex role stereotyping which limit not only the educational and career choices of their students but ultimately the students' entire lives. The stereotyping can be exemplified in the myth of Cinderella and her Prince:

> A young woman will only need to work for a little while—until Prince Charming sweeps her off her feet. She will never have to work or want to work again. She and Prince Charming will live happily ever after until they are both 100 years old at which time they will both die on the same day.[1]

That is the myth. The statistical reality is:
- 54% of all American women between the ages of 18 and 64 are in the labor force;[2]
- 42% of the total American work force are women;[3]
- Even if a woman is married she can expect to work for an average of 25 years (45 years if she is single);[4]
- Even if she has children, she can expect to work. Thirteen million women in the labor force are women with children;[5]
- Even with preschool children, 4.8 million women work;[6]
- One out of 10 of all women in the labor force are presently heads of families and one out of five minority women are heads of families;[7]
- The divorce rate is up 109% since 1962 and rising;[8]
- Fathers by and large contribute less than half the support of children in divided families and enforcement of payment is nearly non-existent;[9]
- The median income of a fully employed woman with a college degree is less than that of a fully employed man with an eighth grade education;[10]
- The longevity rate of women has increased 20.6 years in the last 50 years while the men's rate has increased only 13.8 years;[11]
- Men outnumber women in admissions to mental institutions two to one and have twice as many ulcers;[12] and
- More than two-thirds of the poor over age 65 are women.[13]

These are persuasive statistics. Educators should be aware of them because the numbers are so large that we cannot know *which* of our students will *not* be affected.

Because we cannot guarantee the future of any particular student, it is critical to develop a sex fair educational program which, (1) will encourage serious long-range educational and career planning for girls and young women as independent rather than dependent persons, and (2) will alleviate the pressure and stress experienced by boys and young men because of unrealistic stereotyped expectations and demands which contribute to their high rate of mental and physical illness.

Ingrained attitudes and stereotypes, as well as a genuine unawareness of the damage that is being done to the student locked in a traditional mold, may not fall away at the drop of a statistic. However, workshops can offer an opportunity to check one's own sex role attitudes and expectations from a different perspective. Workshops provide new information and an opportunity to interact in small and large group activities and discussions on the issues raised by the workshop. Under the umbrella of the workshop sanction, participants are offered the freedom to contemplate change and the support to move toward it.

Consciousness Razors

By Verne Moberg

1. Go to a playground in a park and watch some children. Pick one boy and imagine the rest of his life. Make a list of all the things people will tell him he shouldn't do because he's a boy. Then pick a girl and think about how she'll be spending her time from now on. Make a list of all the things everybody will tell her are illegal because she's a girl. Compare the lists. Get up and go over to the boy and girl and give them each a list; tell them it's all right to do all those things.

    Walk home slowly, observing the adults who pass you by.
2. At 11 p.m. on the nineteenth day of every month think about what you've done all day. Next consider what you might have done that day if you had been a man (woman). By January 1 figure out what to do about this.
3. Ask the neighbor girl what she wants to be when she grows up. Then ask her what she would want to be *if she were a boy*. Find her brother and ask him what he wants to be when he grows up. Then ask him what *he* would want to be *if he were a girl*.

    Later, mention to their parents what they said.
4. Force yourself to watch television for six hours. Write down every innuendo you see and hear that denigrates women. Translate all those into insults aimed at midgets. Ask yourself: Would midgets allow that? Would the FCC allow that? Would you allow that if *you* were a midget? If you weren't? If these things offend you, telephone the TV station to let them know, since they say they are interested in public service.
5. Go to your nearest children's library and pick out twenty picture books at random. Page through them and count the number of aprons, checking to see who is wearing each one (males or females, both humans and animals). Go home and count the number of aprons you own. Ask your neighbors how many they own.

    Spend time wondering who is drawing all those aprons, and why?
6. Ask your seven-year-old daughter (or somebody else's) to play this game with you. Just before Christmas, take her down to the toy department of a big department store and go along with her

to visit Santa Claus. When she sits on Santa's knee and he inquires what she wants for Christmas, ask her (in advance) to say: "A set of building blocks and a chemistry set and an electric train and a fire engine." Watch the look on Santa's face. Next go to the toy department of a rival store and this time ask your daughter to tell Santa (as she's sitting on his knee and he asks what she wants): "A Barbie doll and a play kitchen and a toy vacuum sweeper." Check *this* Santa's face.

Afterwards, take your daughter out for an ice cream soda and ask her what she *really* wants for Christmas. Also ask her if she thinks that's right, that people should always get things just on Christmas, and usually only things they're *allowed* to get.

7. Call up your local school board and ask how many girls have won athletic scholarships over the past 10 years? How many boys? If more boys than girls are winning these scholarships, ask if there are other scholarships available to girls, as compensation.

8. Some Saturday morning when everybody in your family has just had a good breakfast and is in a mellow mood, sit down together around the kitchen table and draw up a list of all the fights you have had over the past year (give each one a name and write that down in the first column on a piece of paper). Then write down, for each fight, who was the angriest (in the second column), what that person really wanted to get out of it (third column), how they expressed their anger (fourth column) and finally whether or not they got their way (fifth column).

Then figure out if one style of anger (crying, shouting, fist-pounding, name-calling, pouting, etc.) is more "efficient" in your family than any other. Do the males or the females in the family practice the "efficient" style of anger most frequently?

At this point somebody will accuse the person who drew up the lists of cheating. During the fight that follows, every member of the family should try to express her or his anger in the style that is most efficient for this particular family. The winner gets to make lunch.

9. Ask your kids to ask all their women teachers if they ever wanted to be school administrators.

10. Stand in front of a large mirror together with one or two or three people you are extremely fond of (either males or females, of any age; everybody should be wearing everyday clothes, and preening is prohibited). When everybody is gazing into the mirror, all repeat, in unison: "Mirror, mirror, on the wall, who's the *fairest* of them all?"

Then everybody close their eyes for one minute and listen hard for the mirror's answer.

11. Pick up a copy of *The New York Times* (or any other daily newspaper) for every child in your class (or your family). Give each child one newspaper, one pencil and a slip of paper. Ask everybody to look through the entire newspaper keeping score of how many pictures

there are of men and how many pictures there are of women (both newsphotos and ads). Also, on each picture, ask the children to write down one adjective describing how they think that person felt about having his or her picture taken in that particular way. When everybody's finished, compare results.

If the findings upset you or the children, write a letter to the editor-in-chief of the newspaper reporting on your experiment and ask him/her if he thinks his/her photographers are doing a good job. While you're at it, also ask to have your letter printed along with a reply in the letters-to-the-editor column.

12. This game is called "Meanwhile, back in the kitchen—." It is played in a group of mixed couples (children or adults).

To begin the game the female in the first couple thinks up some great achievement in history performed by a man. For instance: "In 1492 Columbus discovered America." Her male partner must then say what the great man's wife was doing at that particular moment: "Meanwhile, *Mrs.* Columbus was discovering_____." If he does not know what the great man's wife was doing at that moment, he must forfeit and reply: "Meanwhile, back in the kitchen, Mrs. Columbus was doing the dishes" (or fixing supper, or any of those fascinating chores one does in the kitchen). In which case his partner wins the point. The play continues around the room in this fashion until one side (males *or* females) has accumulated 21 points.

Afterwards, the group will want to discuss why they don't know more about what women were doing and how they could go about finding out. Did all those women really spend all that time in the kitchen? If so, should the females now playing the game get extra points?

How did history really happen? In the future, who will be kept in the kitchen?

There is no winner in this game.

Sentence Completions

By David Sadker

(Suggested for use with junior high school students as a follow-up to a discussion of male sex role stereotypes based on "Being a Man: Background for Teachers." pp. 71)

1. A boy who is not good at sports is _____

2. When I see a man teaching in elementary school, I _____

3. Young boys should/should not be allowed to play with dolls because _____

4. The hardest thing about being a boy is _____

5. The best thing about being a boy is _____

6. The last time I remember seeing a man cry was _____

7. A good job for a man is _____

8. Boys should/should not help around the house with cooking and cleaning because _____

9. In general, men do/do not lead happier lives than women because __ _____

10. A sissy is _____

11. A tomboy is _____

12. It is/is not worse for a boy to be a "sissy" than for a girl to be a "tomboy" because _____

Early Socialization

By Barbara Gates, Susan Klaw, and Adria Steinberg

Overview

> My friends called me a tomboy, because I didn't like to play with silly dolls or dress up like they did. I was different. I played with trucks; played baseball, hockey, and basketball with the boys. When my girlfriends saw me doing this they would yell out in front of everyone, "Robbin, you're a tomboy." I would say, "I don't care. Go and play with your silly dolls." And I would finish off what I was doing.
>
> Then I would go home, eat supper, tell my mother what I did all day. Sometimes she would say, "You're a girl, Robbin, not a boy." I didn't care what she said. I would just walk out the door and look for the boys I played with. [Robbin Luzaitis]

This unit explores the ways in which young children learn to be females and males. By focusing on childhood, students begin to comprehend the process by which people are influenced by societal messages. The concept of socialization is difficult to understand, particularly for adolescents, who do not like to think of themselves as unduly influenced by media messages or peer pressures. "Nobody tells me what to think." "I wear what I want to wear." We hear comments like these frequently from our students. It is easier for them to understand how and why children are susceptible to, and influenced by, these messages. A baby, after all, does not know how to act like a girl or a boy—and somehow it learns to do just that.

Through the activities in this unit, students can learn to recognize the ways in which everyone is influenced to take on male and female roles. We start by reading a short story by Lois Gould, "X: A Fabulous Child's Story." This humorous account of Baby X, who is brought up with no sex role messages, is a good introduction to the unit. The struggles the parents go through to protect Baby X from societal messages begin to clarify how socialization usually works. Students then fill out charts on their own families' treatment of them and their brothers. Having remembered what they can of their own experiences, they interview children to see whether things have changed at all. A speaker who teaches children and has observed sex role differences is invited to share her [his] insights as to how and why these differences occur. Finally, the unit ends with students looking at children's books that present traditional sex roles, then, they create their own children's books with new messages.

This unit is brief; it would probably take a class seven to 10 meetings to complete the activities. . . . "Early Socialization" is good introductory material and easily adapted to a coeducational class. It is fun to participate in, and nonthreatening, yet it raises interesting issues.

Activities

1. Bringing Up Baby X

Sex role messages do not begin with comic books or TV. They affect us from the moment of birth. Students learn this quickly when they read "X: A Fabulous Child's Story," by Lois Gould. This is a humorous and interesting fairy tale about Baby X, who, as part of a 23-billion-dollar experiment, was raised to be a child—not a boy or a girl.

> The day the Joneses brought their baby home, lots of friends and relatives came over to see it. None of them knew about the secret experiment, though. So the first thing they asked was what kind of a baby X was. When the Joneses smiled and said, "It's an X," nobody knew what to say. They couldn't say, "Look at her cute little dimples!" And they couldn't say, "Look at his husky little biceps!" And they couldn't even say just plain "kitchy-coo."

The story goes on to outline the difficulties of the Joneses and Baby X in trying to remain free of sex role restrictions. They outrage store clerks, who want to know if it's a girl or boy; passers-by, who look into the baby carriage with the same question; and, finally, parents and administrators at the school Baby X attends, which is "full of rules for boys and girls" but "there were no rules for Xes."

In following the progress of X, the story reveals many of the ways boys and girls are influenced to develop into very different types of people; it suggests areas for further investigation. What makes this reading an especially good way to introduce aspects of early socialization is that it is not presented in a negative way, as a list of increasingly oppressive limitations. The Joneses and Baby X are always in there trying—and in many cases, succeeding—to overcome the traditional sex role boundaries.

This story makes good in-class reading. It is quick reading and amusing enough to hold students' interest to the end. When we have read the story in class, some students have immediately shared stories from their own upbringing—aunts who always pinched their cheeks and told them how adorable they were, teachers who always lined up the girls in front because they know how to be quieter. After finishing the story, the teacher can ask everyone in the class to compare their upbringing to Baby X, to think about the ways they learned (or refused to learn) to act like little girls [or boys]. Encourage the students to be anecdotal, to draw examples from their sisters and brothers, to think back as far as they can.

2. Remembering the Past—Questionnaire on Family and School Influences

Having told a few stories about their early childhood socialization, students fill out a questionnaire and a chart which ask them to think more systematically and in more specific detail about the ways they were brought up.

The questionnaire includes:

1. What did you play with when you were little (toys, games, etc.)? Did you have a bicycle?
2. Whom did you play with?
3. What did you get punished for?
4. Did you learn to cook? sew? clean? If so, who taught you?
5. Did you learn to fix things? take apart motors? etc.?
6. In elementary school, what sports did you participate in? what other games did you play?
7. Did the teachers ever treat boys and girls differently?
8. Now answer all of the above questions as though you were your own brother [sister] (or, if you don't have one, any young boy [girl] you knew well).

The chart looks like this:

What if you. . .
hit a sister or brother
got dirty
got upset and cried
ran around the house
played quietly by yourself
cut school
got a good mark
got a bad mark

What if your brother [sister]. . .

Students may have trouble remembering some of these things. That is to be expected; they should not be made to feel bad about this. Just ask them to fill out as much as they can. If they can't remember things about themselves, ask them to try to fill in with things they've observed about their younger sisters and brothers. When everyone has had a chance to fill out the questionnaire and the chart, the class compares results. You might want to make lists on the board, with "girls" and "boys" as headings.

There is usually some variation in students' responses. A number of people remember childhood as a time when they were allowed more freedom to be "like boys." One student even remarked, "I was a guy when I was a little kid." Up to that point, some of the students in the class had been cold toward her, probably because her direct manner and very casual way of dressing and talking put them off. Seeing this difference in their early socialization helped to explain some of the later style differences and to bring all of the students in the class together.

When we have done this assignment, people have remembered that their parents treated them differently from their brothers with regard to the issues of cleanliness and crying. "When my brother got all dirty, he just had to wash up. When I got dirty, I had to change my clothes. And then my mother would yell at me if I ran out of clothes to change into. She'd keep me in the house." Or, "My mother used to yell at my brother to stop crying and being a sissy." "I could get anything I wanted by crying; I was really spoiled."

It is a good idea to get the students to think about whether this early treatment affects the way people behave later in life. Do they see current effects from their early training to stay clean? Are women generally affected by this need to "keep it clean"? Our students have talked about how their mothers "freak out" at dirt or clutter. A few have mentioned that their mothers do domestic cleaning work for other women. We then ask them to think about jobs that involve getting very dirty and staying dirty—garbage work, mining, ditchdigging. Everyone had seen these jobs as men's work.

A similar discussion about crying led students to admit that they still cry quite a bit, particularly when they want or need sympathy. They were all very aware that this is a general pattern—women tend to cry more readily than men. Because this is such an observable phenomenon, it is a good way to make the connections between early training and adult patterns.

3. Interviews with Young Children

The experience of young children growing up today may be different from the students' own training in sex roles. To see how much things have changed or remained the same, students interview children. The focus is mainly on sex role socialization, but they may also want to ask a few more general questions to get in touch with present-day childrens' perspectives on the world.

Before students design the questionnaire for the interviews, tell them to try to have a specific child in mind. This will help them to think of questions that children can relate to and answer easily. Students almost always enjoy making up questions, especially when these questions are to be asked of their favorite "little people."

1. What do you want to be when you grow up?
2. What are you scared of?
3. What games and toys do you like playing with?
4. Who are your friends? Do you like playing with girls or boys more?
5. If you had one wish, what would it be?
6. Do you like fighting? Whom do you fight with?
7. What are your chores and rules at home?
8. What do you think of school?
9. Do you have a girlfriend? boyfriend?
10. What do you think of teachers?
11. What do you think of police?

12. What do you do that you're not supposed to do?
13. Do you ever get into trouble? For what?

Students can create a list of questions like these in about 20 minutes. Each should then be asked to think of one girl and one boy under 10 she could interview. The names and ages of targeted interviewees are listed on the board. If possible, there should be an age range, with at least one-quarter of the interviewees six years old or under.

The simplest system [to handle interview results] is to list the questions on one side of the blackboard, and place the categories "Girls" and "Boys" at the top of the board. We have found that even more interesting comparisons are possible when there are four categories, by age and sex; i.e., "Girls under Six," "Boys under Six," "Girls Six to Ten," "Boys Six to Ten."

As each person gives their interview results, there is often a high level of interest in the class. The students like to hear what the little children had to say for themselves; many of the answers are amusing or unexpected. "What are you most scared of?" "My big brother!" "Fish eyes!!" "Ghosts!" "One Wish?" "To be able to beat up my older brother." "A Snoopy radio." "All the money in the world."

In looking for girl/boy patterns, it is best to start with the questions regarding the future and chores at home. On the question, "What do you want to be when you grow up?" our students got such results from the girls as: nurse, married, a mother, a teacher; and from the boys: basketball player, cowboy, cop, fireman. Although our students expected to find differences in aspirations between boys and girls, they were surprised by the definitiveness of these results. There wasn't one little girl, under six or over, who thought of herself in a traditionally male role, or one little boy who could imagine himself in a traditionally female role.

A marked differentiation also occurred around household chores. The little girls interviewed (particularly those six and over) all had tasks like setting the table, helping mother clean, making beds, doing dishes. The little boys (under and over six) often had no chores at all—or just taking out the trash. This brought forth a number of angry responses from students who remembered all too well the unfairness of that division of labor in the home.

The questions about school and teachers also elicited sex-differentiated responses, with age an additional factor. The girls of all ages had more favorable attitudes toward school and teachers than the boys, although the younger boys' responses were very similar to those of the girls.

A good summary for this activity is to ask the students whether they were surprised by any of the answers from the children. "Were the children interviewed like you, or different from you, at that age?"

4. Speaker on Sex Role Patterns

If an appropriate speaker can be found, students might enjoy comparing what they have found from their interviews with the observations of someone who works with young children every day. Through your own personal contacts, or through students or parents who work as aides in day care centers or kindergartens, you can probably find speakers who have a great deal to say about the differences in behavior of young girls and boys.

These speakers should be asked to tell about their experiences, focusing on the ways boys and girls act differently, reasons why this might be so, and examples of how they have tried to overcome some of these differences. Specific questions to ask a speaker include:

1. Do boys and girls play with the same kinds of toys?
2. Do boys and girls play more together, or separately?
3. Do boys and girls dress differently? Does this affect their play?
4. Are the teachers closer to the boys or to the girls?
5. Do girls or boys give up faster when something is hard to do?
6. Do girls fight with each other? Do boys? Do girls and boys fight with each other? Who starts fights?
7. Do the girls or boys act any differently when their parents are around?
8. Do any of these patterns change as the kids get older?

In looking for a speaker to answer these and related questions, it is more important to find someone who speaks the students' language and tunes in quickly to their interests, than to find a professional with a great deal of expertise. The point is to bring in someone who has daily classroom experience with young boys and girls, who is aware of the processes of sex role socialization, and who has ideas about moving beyond traditional role boundaries.

5. Children's Books

In this activity, students move from examining and interpreting sex-role messages to creating their own. This is an important step to take. In the first two units, they see themselves, other people their age, and young children mainly as the passive recipients of these official messages. Now, in designing children's books, they are in the positions of influencing other people. They have to figure out what messages they want children to receive.

This activity begins with students briefly looking over some children's books that present traditional sex roles. The teacher can find a sampling of these books in any children's library or school library; students can also be asked to bring such books from their homes. *I'm Glad I'm a Boy, I'm Glad I'm a Girl*, by Whitney Darrow Jr., and the *When I Grow Up* series, by Jean Bethell, are especially suitable for this purpose. There are numerous others that show typical American families divided into the typical male/female roles for adults and children.

. . . Each student goes through one or two books, answering the following questions:

1. Is the main character a girl or boy?
2. How does she or he look? What does he or she wear?
3. What does the main character do, or what happens to her/him?
4. What is the main character interested in?
5. What kind of personality does the main character have?
6. Are there adults in the book? If so, who are they?
7. What are the adult women shown doing, saying, thinking, etc.?
8. What are adult men shown doing, saying, thinking, etc.?
9. What messages would a young girl reading this book get? A young boy?

It is possible to use a simpler format. Each student makes four lists: "Boys," "Girls," "Men," "Women." Under each heading, the student describes how these characters look, what they are shown doing or thinking, how they behave, etc.

Typical patterns emerge. Often girls are shown sitting, waiting patiently, watching. The more active ones might be playing with their dolls, cooking, helping mommy, or tagging along behind their brothers. Boys are pictured as having a more adventurous, active young life; climbing trees, playing sports, getting into mischief. Women are mostly mothers, housewives, maids, cooks, or occasionally, secretaries or nurses. Men are shown hurrying off to work, coming home at night to enjoy a family life, or taking their children out on the weekend. All of these are easy to pick out, in both the text and the pictures.

By now, none of this is new or surprising to the students. They have looked at enough magazines and TV, and have talked enough about societal messages to know what to expect. But we have found that for many students it was the children's books that drove the point home. Even though they could see sex role messages in the media, they could not quite comprehend the extent to which they could affect people. It is easier to accept the susceptibility of children to these messages; it is more obvious that children's books are a form of indoctrination.

Having acquired the skill of finding and labeling sex-role messages, students are now asked to use their imaginations to create their own children's books. We usually start them off with the directive to try to make up a story that will be different from the ones they have read and that will picture different kinds of young girls and boys. We ask them to think about what choices they would like to see open to their younger brothers and sisters. For students with more advanced writing skills, we might suggest changing a familiar fairy tale to make new points.

If anyone has a hard time coming up with an idea, we show her [him] some new, alternative children's books to suggest approaches. (For example, every issue of *Ms.* has "Stories for Free Children"; The Feminist Press and Lollipop Power have put out series of liberating children's books.) But most people are able to draw upon experiences in their own lives. A student whose mother is a waitress who has taught herself carpentry in her spare time wrote "A Girl's Dream." This is the story of Lisa, who wants to be a carpenter, even though her brothers tell her to "go play with your dolls." With her mother's support, she studies carpentry in school, makes a beautiful bookcase, and wins the first prize in a woodworking contest—her own tool box. Other titles have included: "Melvin Wants to Be a Nurse," "My Only Best Brother," "Little Jack Riding Hood," "Baseball Is My Favorite Sport!" and "Emily Has Nine Wishes."

The students begin by choosing a topic and writing the rough draft of a story. In writing, they should keep in mind that they will want to illustrate it later. The teacher then goes over the draft with each student, trying to make the stories ready for "publication." The desire to produce complete, attractive children's books motivates the students to do careful corrections on their stories. It is a good chance to work with them on common spelling and grammatical mistakes.

The next step in the process is dividing the copy into short sections and then illustrating those sections. Looking at published children's books may help students get ideas for layout and illustrations. They should be reassured that the drawings can be very simple; even stick figures tell the story. Sometimes the students get so attached to their stories that they really want excellent illustrations, and they ask artistic friends to do these. We neither encourage nor discourage this. The point is for the students to use their creativity and to feel good about the finished products.

Reading over the finished books together serves two purposes. First, it gives everyone a sense of pride in their work and a collective sense of accomplishment. Second, each author can receive feedback about the sex role messages conveyed by her [his] book. After each student shows her [his] book to the class, other students give their impressions of the messages. This gives everyone in the class a reason for listening carefully to each student's writing. Next, the author herself [himself] explains what she [he] intended the messages to be. She [he] has a chance to see whether she [he] accomplished what she [he] intended.

This process has resulted in some interesting discussions and, occasionally, in students' changing their stories. "Baseball Is My Favorite Sport" is about Judy, who thought "playing school, house, dolls, and mother were boring." Instead, she wished that "her brother Joey and the rest of the boys would let her play baseball." In the original version of the story, Judy's mother takes her to a psychiatrist (Dr. Elizabeth Reed), who reassures the mother that "this is all right now—that it is just a stage."

In the discussion, the author realized that the message people took away from the story was that girls outgrow their interest in sports. Her intention had been to make readers feel that it's good for girls to play baseball and that parents should support them in that desire.

In the rewritten version, the book concludes:

> In fact, she [the psychiatrist] said that it was quite normal for Judy to play baseball and girls should play just as much as boys. So that afternoon, Judy's mother took her

downtown to the department store and bought her a ball, bat, and glove to practice in her yard. [Colleen Long]

A good follow-up to this activity is to visit a day care center or kindergarten where the students will be allowed to read their children's books to the children. They can then see firsthand how children respond . to their stories.

Consciousness-Raising Activities For Sixth-Grade Students

By Marilyn Roessler

I. Goals

A. To create student awareness of what stereotyping is and to help them relate this concept to their own attitudes.
B. To make students aware of sexist attitudes and practices in their school and community.
C. To have students develop a method of bringing these issues to other sixth-grade students.

II. Project Description

A. The students first took a vocabulary quiz of words pertaining to sex discrimination. Some of the words included were "sexist," "discrimination," "prejudice," and "stereotype."
B. The girls wrote an essay beginning, "If I were a boy, I would . . . ." Boys wrote one entitled, "If I were a girl, I would . . . ."
C. Next students wrote an essay entitled, "Myself an Adult, Not Married . . . ." in which they were instructed to envision themselves at some stage of adult life.
D. The next activity was developed by the sponsor to make students aware of how stereotyped our images often are. Fifty descriptive words were put on the overhead projector; the students were asked to determine whether the words described boys, girls, football players, clergy, or movie stars. A heated discussion ensued as students decided which categories these words fit in (for results, see Addendum).
E. Students were asked to bring in magazine pictures which represented a stereotype of an individual or an activity. The class was divided into small groups and each prepared a collage using pictures it had collected.
F. The culminating activity was to have each student submit questions to include on an awareness questionnaire for other sixth-graders.

III. Evaluation

A. The initial response to the vocabulary test indicated a lack of knowledge of this area. Only three of the 50 students knew the meaning of the word"stereotype."
   1. As the activities progressed, the project sponsor felt the students began to understand the meaning and implications of a stereotype.
   2. By the end of the project, all students had become aware of their own attitudes and understood the concept of a stereotype.
B. The essay writing exercise was successful because it evoked student enthusiasm and brought forth revealing insights.
   1. In the essay "Myself, an Adult . . . ," most girls saw themselves in traditional female roles, even though they did not portray themselves as married. Some of the occupations were nurse, teacher, bakery salesgirl, clerical worker, and stewardess.
      a. Some saw themselves as not engaged in any work.
      b. Some thought their jobs would pay poorly.
      c. One saw herself as a lawyer, but plagued by prejudice.
      d. Another saw herself as a veterinarian, but believed she would encounter financial problems in running her own hospital.
   2. Male essays on the same subject indicated a strong sense of direction, accomplishment, and confidence in themselves, both monetarily and professionally.
      a. Occupations boys listed included architecture, medicine, statistics, professional athletics, and law.
      b. Boys believed they would be financially successful. If they had monetary problems, they would be able to solve them.
   3. In the essays "If I were a Boy," girls indicated they would
      a. engage in more athletics
      b. have closer relationships with fathers
      c. not be resentful of being males.
   4. The boys said that if they were girls, they would
      a. be good students
      b. be physically attractive
      c. feel it is unfortunate to be a girl (a comment from over half the boys).
C. The least successful activity was the questionnaire design: This proved to be too difficult because most of the students wrote similar questions; the results were not useful.

IV. Recommendations

A. Part of the success of this project is attributable to several key factors:
   1. The project was done with two classes and two teachers (although the project sponsor was clearly in charge of the activities with the other teacher assisting her).
   2. The range and liveliness of the discussions was increased by the heterogenous grouping of the students.

3. The students were given essay assignments prior to any discussions; thus they were provided with an opportunity to reveal some of their own ideas and attitudes before being exposed to any "new" ideas or information.
4. Each of the activities was short enough to maintain the students' interest and different enough from the previous one so that the students were not bored.
5. The progression of the activities beginning with student realization of their own ideas to an examination of the ideas and attitudes of society allowed the students to see the link between the two.

B. All these activities can be modified for use with different age groups. They are easy to do, do not cost any money to implement, and are stimulating for both the students and the teachers.
   1. Because of the flexibility of these activities, they can be grouped into a mini-course, spread out over a marking period, or the entire year.
   2. Once the students have become excited about these activites, it would be good to reinforce this enthusiasm by having them suggest additional exercises to expand on the basic concepts.

C. It would be valuable for any district duplicating this project to include students in the planning phases. These students could also pre-test some of the activities and provide valuable feedback for the project sponsor.

D. An evaluation component should be built into the project so that the sponsor and staff will have an indication from students of the most valuable activities. It will also give them the opportunity to reflect on the experience and to acknowledge what new information they obtained, how their attitudes have changed, and what other activities they feel would be useful.

ADDENDUM

Stereotyped

Boys	*Girls*
rough	fragile
show-off	talkative
athletic	unpredictable
carefree	long nails
lazy	willful
conceited	temper
brave	giggly
rugged	modest
strong	wayward
messy	graceful
egotistic	long hair
short hair	weak
clumsy	smart
	neat
	creative

Football Players	Ministers, Rabbis, Priests	Movie Stars
rough	religious	rich
big	weak	sexy
strong	smart	egotistical
smelly	quiet	phony
fat	holy	funny
dumb	active	show-off
fast	robes	glamorous
husky	serious	talented
show-off	good	envious
aggressive	kind	carefree
muscular	somber	gay
active	pleasant	
	fatherly	

Footnotes and References

Forms of Sex Bias and Their Manifestations in the Classroom

[1] National Assessment of Educational Progress, "Males Dominate in Educational Success," *NAEP Newsletter*. October 1975.

[2] Robert Spaulding, "Achievement, Creativity, and Self-Concept Correlates of Teacher-Pupil Interactions in Elementary School," Cooperative Research Project No. 1352. Washington, D.C.: U.S. Department of Health, Education, and Welfare, Office of Education, 1963.

[3] C. S. Dweck, "Sex Differences in the Meaning of Negative Evaluation in Achievement Situations: Determinants and Consequences," paper presented at the annual meeting of the Society for Research in Child Development. Denver, Colorado, 1975.

[4] V. C. Crandall, "Sex Differences in Expectancy of Intellectual and Academic Reinforcement," in C. P. Smith (eds.), *Achievement Related Motives in Children*. New York: Russell Sage Foundation, 1969.

[5] L. Serbin, K. O'Leary, and I. Tonick, "A Comparison of Teacher Responses to the Pre-Academic and Problem Behavior of Boys and Girls," *Child Development* 44 (1973): pp. 796-804.

[6] Robert Rosenthal and Lenore Jacobson, "Pygmalion in the Classroom: An Excerpt," in Melvin Silberman (ed.), *The Experience of Schooling*. New York: Holt, Rinehart and Winston, 1971.

[7] Carl Braun, "Teacher Expectation: Sociopsychological Dynamics," *Review of Educational Research* 46: pp. 185-213, Spring 1976.

[8] B. J. Kemes, "A Study of the Relationship Between the Sex of the Student and the Assignment of Marks by Secondary School Teachers," Ph.D. dissertation, Michigan State University, 1965.

[9] Michael Palardy, "For Johnny's Reading Sake," *Reading Teacher* 22: pp. 720-724, May 1969.

[10] Carl Braun, *op. cit.*, p. 209.

[11] Carol Jacklin, "Sex Differences," paper prepared for Resource Center on Sex Roles in Education. Washington, D.C., 1977.

[12] Patricia Gillespie and Albert Fink, "The Influence of Sexism on the Education of Handicapped Children," *Exceptional Children* 41: p. 159, November 1974.

Sexism in Language: The Case for Including Everybody

Bem, S. L., and Bem, D. J."Does Sex-biased Job Advertising Aid and Abet Sex Discrimination?" *Journal of Applied Social Psychology* 3:6-18; 1973.

Bosmajian, M. A. "The Language of Sexism," *ETC: A Review of General Semantics* 29:305-12; September 1972.

Burr, E.; Dunn, S.; and Farquhar, N."Women and the Language of Inequality." *Social Education* 36:841-45; December 1972.

Ernst, S. H. B. *An Investigation of Students' Interpretation of Inclusionary and Exclusionary Gender Generic Language.* Unpublished doctoral dissertation. Pullman: Washington State University, 1977.

Harrison, L. "Cro-Magnon Women—In Eclipse." *The Science Teacher* 42:8-11; April 1975.

Harrison, L., and Passero, R. N. "Sexism in the Language of Elementary School Textbooks." *Science and Children* 2:22-25; January 1975.

Key, M. R. "Linguistic Behavior of Male and Female." *Linguistics* 88:15-31; August 1972.

Kidd, V. "A Study of the Images Produced Through the Use of the Male Pronoun as the Generic." *Moments in Contemporary Rhetoric and Communication* 1:25-29; Fall 1971.

Lakoff, R. "Language and Women's Place." *Language in Society* 2:45-80; 1972.

Russell, L. M. "Changing Language and the Church." *The Liberating Word: A Guide to Non-sexist Interpretation of the Bible.* (Edited by L. M. Russell). Philadelphia: Westminster Press, 1976. pp. 82-98.

Schneider, J., and Hacker, S. "Sex Role Imagery and Use of the Generic Man in Introductory Tests: A Case in the Sociology of Sociology." *American Sociologist* 8:12-18; 1972.

Tiedt, I. "Sexism in Language, An Editor's Plague." *Elementary English* 50:1073-74; October 1973.

Images of Males and Females in Elementary School Textbooks in Five Subject Areas

[1] The sample was drawn from the teacher associations in each of these areas, faculty at educational and research institutions, and the publishers of textbooks mentioned as leaders in the field. In each subject area we tried to determine the books with the largest sales and usage pattern over the five-year period from 1967 to 1972.

[2] The consensus on the most widely used series varied greatly by discipline. In spelling there was almost complete agreement, and the McGraw Hill series "Basic Goals and Spelling" was used. In science the Harcourt Brace series "Concepts in Science" was used. In mathematics the Houghton Mifflin series, "Modern School Mathematics Structure and Use," was analyzed. In reading two series appeared equal, and both were used in the analysis. These were Scott Foresman's series "New Basic Readers," and Ginn and Co.'s "Basic Readers—100 Edition." In social studies, we found the least amount of consensus, as the field was undergoing major change. We therefore deviated from our established pattern and chose a newer series, Harcourt Brace's "The Social Sciences—Concepts and Values," which appeared to be capturing the current market.

[3] Mothers, however, conform to the textbook norm of domestic women and are not active. The only women in textbooks who are active are aunts and grandmothers—women who have no children of their own or who are beyond the childbearing age—as if the textbooks have to dichotomize the role of mother from those roles which show women as active and energetic people.

Sexual Stereotyping and Mathematics Learning

Astin, H. S. "Sex Differences in Mathematical and Scientific Precocity." In *Mathematical Talent: Discovery, Description and Development,* edited by J. C. Stanley, D. P. Keating, and L. Fox, pp. 70-87. Baltimore, Md.: Johns Hopkins University Press, 1974.

Carnegie Commission on Higher Education. *Opportunities for Women in Higher Education.* New York: McGraw-Hill Book Co., 1973.

Crandall, V. J., W. Katkovsky, and A. Preston. "Motivational and Ability Determinants of Young Children's Intellectual Achievement Behaviors." *Child Development* 33 (1962): 643-61.

Fennema, E. "Mathematics Learning and the Sexes: A Review." *Journal for Research in Mathematics Education* 5: 126-39; May 1974.

———. "Spatial Ability. Mathematics, and the Sexes." In *Mathematics Learning: What Research Says about Sex Differences*, edited by E. Fennema. Columbus, Ohio: ERIC Center for Science, Mathematics, and Environmental Education, College of Education, The Ohio State University, 1975.

Fennema, E. and J. Sherman (a). "Sex-Related Differences in Mathematics Achievement, Spatial Visualization and Affective Factors." Manuscript submitted for publication, 1976.

——— (b). "Sex-Related Differences in Mathematics Achievement and Related Factors: A Further Study." Manuscript submitted for publication, 1976.

Hilton, T. L., and G. W. Berglund, *Sex Differences in Mathematics Achievement—A Longitudinal Study.* Princeton, N.J.: Educational Testing Service, 1971.

Horner, M. "Achievement-related Conflicts in Women." In *New Perspectives on Women, Journal of Social Issues,* edited by M. Mednick and S. Tangri, 28 (1972): 157-75.

Kagan, J. "Acquisition and Significance of Sex Typing and Sex Role Identity." In *Review of Child Development Research,* edited by M. L. Hoffman and L. W. Hoffman, pp. 137-67. New York: Russell Sage Foundation, 1964.

Maccoby, E. E., and C. N. Jacklin, "Sex Differences in Intellectual Functioning." In *Assessment in a Pluralistic Society,* proceedings of the Invitational Conference on Testing Problems, Princeton, N.J.: Educational Testing Services, 1973.

———. *Psychology of Sex Differences.* Palo Alto, Calif.: Stanford University, 1974.

Mullis, I. V. S. *Educational Achievement and Sex Discrimination.* Denver: National Assessment of Educational Progress, 1975.

Sherman, J. A. "Problem of Sex Differences in Space Perception and Aspects of Intellectual Functioning." *Psychological Review* 74: 290-99; April 1967.

Sherman, J. A., and E. Fennema. "Distribution of Spatial Visualization and Mathematical Problem Solving Scores." Manuscript submitted for publication, 1976.

Stafford, R. E. "Hereditary and Environmental Components of Quantitative Reasoning." *Review of Educational Research* 42: 183-201; February 1972.

Stein, A. H., and M. M. Bailey. "The Socialization of Achievement Orientation in Females." *Psychological Bulletin* 80: 345-66; May 1973.

Stein, A. H., and J. Smithells. "Age and Sex Differences in Children's Sex-Role Standards about Achievement." *Developmental Psychology* 1: 252-59; March 1969.

Williams, T. "Family Resemblances in Abilities: The Wechsler Scales." *Behavior Genetics* 5 (1975): 405-9.

Why Don't Girls Misbehave More Than Boys in School?

Abel, H., and Gingles, R. (1965). "Identifying Problems of Adolescent Girls." *Journal of Educational Research* 58: 389-392.

Adams, J. P. (1964). "Adolescent Personal Problems as a Function of Age and Sex. *Journal of Genetic Psychology* 104: 207-214.

Albert, N., and Beck, A. T. (1975). "Incidence of Depression in Early Adolescence: A Preliminary Study." *Journal of Youth Adolescence* 4: 301-307.

Amos, R. T., and Washington, R. M. (1960). "A Comparison of Pupil and Teacher Perceptions of Pupil Problems. *Journal of Educational Psychology* 51: 255-258.

Astin, H. S. (1975). "Young Women and Their Roles." In Havighurst, R. J., and Dreyer, P. H. (eds.), *Youth, Seventy-Fourth Yearbook of the National Society for the Study of Education, Part 1.* Chicago: University of Chicago Press, 1975; pp. 419-434.

Buros, O. K. (ed.) (1972). *The Seventh Mental Measurements Yearbook.* Highland Park, N.J.: Gryphon Press.

Campbell, M. M., and Cooper, K. (1975). "Parents' Perception of Adolescent Behavior Problems." *Journal of Youth and Adolescence* 4: 309-320.

Cavior, H. E., Hayes, S. C., and Cavior, N. (1975). "Physical Attractiveness of Female Offenders." In Brodsky, A. M. (eds.), *The Female Offender,* SAGE Contemporary Social Science Issues, No. 19. Beverly Hills, Calif.: SAGE Publications, 1975. pp. 29-39.

Clements, H. M., and Delke, M. C. (1967). "Factors Related to Reported Problems of Adolescents." *Personnel and Guidance Journal* 45: 697-702.

Cole, C. W., Oetting, E. R., and Miskimins, R. W. (1969). "Self-concept Therapy for Adolescent Females." *Journal of Abnormal Psychology.* 74: 642-645.

Coleman, J. S. (1961). *The Adolescent Society.* New York: Free Press.

Conger, J. J. (1973). *Adolescence and Youth.* New York: Harper & Row.

Cottle, W. C. (1972). "Identifying Potential Delinquents in Junior High School." *Meas. Eval. Guid.* 5: 271-276.

Cusick, P. A. (1973). *Inside High School.* New York: Holt, Rinehart and Winston.

Damico, S. B. (1976). "Clique Membership and its Relationship to Academic Achievement and Attitude Toward School." *Journal of Research and Development in Education* 9: 29-35.

Duke, D. L. (1976). "Who Misbehaves?—A High School Studies its Discipline Problems." *Education Administration Quarterly* 12: 65-85.

Duke, D. L. (1978). "How Administrators View the 'Crisis' in School Discipline." *Phi Delta Kappan* 59: 325-330.

Duke, D. L., and Duke, P. M. (1978). "The Prediction of Delinquency in Girls." *Journal of Research and Development in Education* 11: 18-33.

Garrison, K. C., and Cunningham, B. W. (1952). "Personal Problems of Ninth-grade Pupils." *School Review* 60: 30-33.

Gold, M. (1970). *Delinquent Behavior in an American City.* Belmont, Calif.: Brooks-Cole Publishing Company.

Gold, M., and Reimer, D. J. (1972). *Changing Patterns of Delinquent Behavior Among Americans 13 Through 16 Years Old: 1967-1972.* National Survey of Youth Report, No. 1. Ann Arbor: University of Michigan Research Center for Group Dynamics.

Good, T. W., and Brophy, J. E. (1974). "Changing Teacher and Student Behavior: An Empirical Investigation." *Journal of Educational Psychology* 66: 390-405.

Gregg, G. (1976). "High School—A Tough Place for Girls." *Psychology Today* 10:36–37.

Hampe, E., Miller, L., Barrett, C., and Noble, H. (1973). "Intelligence and School Phobia." *Journal of School Psychology* 11: 66-70.

Harper, J., and Colling, J. K. (1975). "A Differential Survey of the Problems of Privileged and Underprivileged Adolescents." *Journal of Youth and Adolescence* 4: 349-358.

Hayes, M. L. (1943). *A Study of the Classroom Disturbances of Eighth Grade Boys and Girls,* Bureau of Publications. New York: Teachers College, Columbia University.

Heinstein, M. (1969). *Behavior Problems of Young Children in California,* N.C.:N.P.

Hindelang, M. J. (1976). "With a Little Help from Their Friends: Group Participation in Reported Delinquent Behaviour." *British Journal of Criminology* 16: 109-125.

Hofmann, A. D. (1975). "Adolescents in Distress." Symposium of Adolescent Medicine. *Medical Clinics of North America* 59: 1429-1437.

Jackson, P. W. (1968). *Life in Classrooms.* New York: Holt, Rinehart and Winston.

Kelly, D. H. (1976). "Track Position, School Misconduct, and Youth Deviance." *Urban Education* 10: 379-388.

Khleif, B. B. (1964). "Teachers as Predictors of Juvenile Delinquency and Psychiatric Disturbance." *Social Problems* 11: 270-282.

Kratcoski, P. C., and Kratcoski, J. E. (1975). "Changing Patterns in the Delinquent Activities of Boys and Girls: A Self-reported Delinquency Analysis." *Adolescence* 10: 83-91.

Liddle, G. (1958). "The California Psychological Inventory and Certain Social and Personal Factors." *Journal of Educational Psychology* 49: 144-149.

Maccoby, E. E. (ed.) (1966). *The Development of Sex Differences.* Stanford, Calif.: Stanford University Press.

McPartland, J. M., and McDill, E. L. (1976). *The Unique Role of Schools in the Causes of Youthful Crime,* Report No. 216. Center for Social Organization of Schools. Baltimore: The Johns Hopkins University.

Ostrov, E., Offer, D., Marohn, R. C., and Rosenwein, T. (1972). "The 'Impulsivity index': Its Application to Juvenile Delinquency." *Journal of Youth and Adolescence* 1: 179-196.

Peterson, D. R. (1961). "Behavior Problems of Middle Childhood. *Journal of Consulting Psychology* 25: 205-209.

Porteus, S. D. (1968). "New Applications of the Porteus Maze Tests." *Perceptual and Motor Skills* 26: 787-798.

Richards, C. V. (1966). "Discontinuities in Role Expectations of Girls." In W. W. Wattenberg (ed.), *Social Deviancy Among Youth, Sixty-fifth Yearbook of the National Society for the Study of Education, Part 1.* Chicago: University of Chicago Press. pp. 164-188.

Rist, R. (1970). "Student Social Class and Teacher Expectations: The Self-fulfilling Prophecy in Ghetto Education." *Harvard Education Review* 40: 411-451.

Schutz, R. E. (1958). "Patterns of Personal Problems of Adolescent Girls. *Journal of Educational Psychology* 49: 1-5.

Serbin, L. A., O'Leary, K. D., Kent, R. N., and Tonick, I. J. (1973). "A Comparison of Teacher Response to the Pre-academic and Problem Behavior of Boys and Girls." *Child Development* 44: 796-804.

Silberberg, N. E., and Silberberg, M. C. (1971). "School Achievement and Delinquency. *Review of Educational Research* 41: 17-33.

Simmons, R. G., and Rosenberg, F. (1975). "Sex, Sex Roles, and Self-image. *Journal of Youth and Adolescence* 4: 229-258.

Smith, I. L., and Greenberg, S. (1975). "Teacher Attitudes and the Labeling Process." *Exceptional Children* 41: 319-324.

Stanton, M. (1974). "The Concept of Conflict at Adolescence." *Adolescence* 9: 537-546.

Stein, A. H., and Friedrich, L. K. (1975). "The Effects of Television Content on Young Children." In Pick, A. D. (ed.), *Minnesota Symposia on Child Psychology,* Vol. IX. Minneapolis: University of Minnesota Press, pp. 78-105.

Stern, H., and Grosz, H. J. (1969). "H.S.P.Q. Personality Measurements of Institutionalized Delinquent Girls and Their Temporal Stability." *Journal of Clinical Psychology* 25: 289-292.

Thompson, R. J., and Lozes, J. (1976). "Female Gang Delinquency." *Corrective Social Psychology* 22:1-5.

Wiggins, R. G. (1973). "Differences in Self-perceptions of Ninth Grade Boys and Girls." *Adolescence* 8: 491-496.

Zeitlin, H. (1955). "Disciplinary Problems Reported by Teachers in a Metropolitan High School System." Unpublished doctoral dissertation, Stanford University.

Being a Man: Background for Teachers

[1] N. Frazier and M. Sadker. *Sexism in School and Society*. New York: Harper & Row, 1973.

[2] D. G. Brown. "Sex Role Preference in Young Children." *Psychological Monographs* 70 (1956). See also D. G. Brown, "Sex Role Development in Young Children." *Psychological Bulletin* 54 (1958): 232-242. See also L. B. Fauls and W. D. Smith. "Sex Role Learning of Five-Year-Olds." *Journal of Genetic Psychology* 93 (1958): 133-148.

[3] Marc Feigen Fasteau. *The Male Machine*. New York: McGraw-Hill, 1974.

[4] Eleanor Maccoby and Carol Jacklin. *The Psychology of Sex Differences*. Stanford, Calif.: Stanford University Press, 1974. p. 399.

[5] Carol A. Dwyer. "Sex Differences in Reading: An Evaluation and a Critique of Current Theories." *Review of Educational Research* 43: 462-465, Fall 1973.

[6] Robert Fein. "Men's Experiences Before and After the Birth of a First Child: Dependence, Marital Sharing, and Anxiety" (doctoral dissertation, Harvard University, 1974).

[7] Jack Nichols, *Men's Liberation*. New York: Penguin Books, 1975.

[8] Lee Firester and Joan Firester. "Wanted: A New Deal for Boys." *The Elementary School Journal*. October 1974.

[9] Sandra Lipsitz Bem. "Androgyny vs. the Tight Little Lives of Fluffy Women and Chesty Men." *Psychology Today*. September 1975, pp. 59-62.

Title IX of the Education Amendments, 1972

[1] 20 U.S.C. §1681 *et seq*. (Supp. IV, 1974).

[2] 40 Fed. Reg. 24137 (1975) (to be codified at 45 C.F.R. Part 86). Included next in this handbook.

[3] 20 U.S.C. §1681(a) (6) (Supp. IV, 1974) exempts fraternities and sororities from the provisions of Title IX.

Title IX and Grievance Procedures

[1] The terms "complaint" and "grievance" are used apparently interchangeably within §86.8 of the regulation to implement Title IX. This manual shall follow the regulation of this interchangeable usage: an allegation of noncompliance with Title IX made within the structure of an internal procedure shall be referred to as either a "complaint" or a "grievance." An allegation of noncompliance which is filed with the Office for Civil Rights, HEW, shall be referred to as a "federal complaint."

The Why of a Workshop

[1] Verheyden-Hilliard, Mary Ellen. "Sexism—Does What You Can't See Hurt You?" *Student Advocate*, National Association of Secondary School Principals, 2(7), March 1975.

[2] U.S. Department of Labor, Employment Standards Administration, Women's Bureau. *Women in the Labor Force*. Washington, D.C.: August 1974–75.

[3] U.S. Department of Labor, Women's Bureau. Washington, D.C.: December 1979.

[4] U.S. Department of Labor, Employment Standards Administration, Women's Bureau. *The Myth and the Reality*. Washington, D.C.: May 1974 (revised).

[5] U.S. Department of Labor, Employment Standards Administration, Women's Bureau.

Highlights of Women's Employment and Education. Washington, D.C.: June 1974 (revised).

[6] Ibid.

[7] U.S. Department of Labor, Employment Standards Administration, Women's Bureau. *Twenty Facts on Women Workers.* Washington, D.C.: June 1974.

[8] U.S. Department of Health, Education and Welfare, National Center for Health Statistics. *Provisional Statistics 1974.* Rockville, Md.

[9] Citizens' Advisory Council on the Status of Women, Department of Labor. *The Equal Rights Amendments Alimony and Child Support Laws.* Washington, D.C.: January 1972.

[10] U.S. Department of Labor, Employment Standards Administration, Women's Bureau. *The Earning Gap: Median Earnings of Year-round Full-time Workers, by Sex.* Washington, D.C.: March 1975.

[11] U.S. Department of Commerce, Bureau of the Census. *Provisional Statistics 1974.* Washington, D.C.

[12] U.S. Department of Health, Education and Welfare, National Institute of Mental Health, Biometrics Division. *Sex Ratio of the Male to Female Admission Rate to State and County Mental Hospitals,* United States, in *Statistical Note 97,* Table 4, p. 7. Rockville, Md.: September 1973.

U.S. Department of Health, Education and Welfare, Center for Health Statistics, Division of Health Survey-Interview Statistics, #1083. *Survey of Incidence of Stomach Ulcers in Males and Females in 1968.* Rockville, Md.: September 1973.

[13] U.S. Senate, Special Committee on Aging. *Women and Social Security: Adapting to a New Era.* Washington, D.C.: October 27, 1975.

Selected References

Adams, Ruth. *A Woman's Place*. New York: W. W. Norton & Co., Inc., 1977

Ahlum, Carol, and Fralley, Jacqueline M. *High School Feminist Studies*. Old Westbury, N.Y.: Feminist Press, 1976.

Alfrey, Jean. *Equal Rights for Women in Education: A Resource Handbook for Policy Makers*. Denver, Col.: Education Commission of the States, Equal Rights for Women in Education Project, 1976.

American Association of University Women. *Tool Catalog: Techniques and Strategies for Successful Action Programs*. Washington, D.C., the Association. 252 pp. 1978.

Barber, Elinor G. "Some International Perspectives on Sex Differences in Education."*Signs: Journal of Women in Culture and Society*, Spring 1977. pp. 584-92.

Berk. L. E., and Lewis, N. G. "Sex Role and Social Behavior in Four School Environments." *Elementary School Journal* 77:204-17; January 1977.

Bickel, P. J., and others. "Sex Bias in Graduate Admissions: Data from Berkeley." *Science* 187:398-404; February 7, 1975.

Blaxall, Martha, and Reagan, Barbara R., eds. *Women and the Workplace: The Implications of Occupational Segregation*. Chicago: University of Chicago Press, 1976.

Bullough, Vern, and Bullough, Bonnie. *The Subordinate Sex: A History of Attitudes Toward Women*. Urbana: University of Illinois Press, 1973.

Cardenas, Blandina, and Cardenas, J. A. "Chicano: Bright-Eyed, Bilingual, Brown, and Beautiful." *Today's Education* 62:49-51; February 1973.

Carney, Clarke G., and McMahon, S. Lynne. *Exploring Contemporary Male-Female Roles: A Facilitator's Guide*. San Diego, Calif.: University Associates, 1977.

Chafe, William H. *Women & Equality: Changing Patterns in American Culture*. Fairlawn, N.J.: Oxford University Press, 1977.

Chapman, Jane R., and Gates, Margaret. *Women Into Wives: The Legal & Economic Impact of Marriage*. (Yearbooks in Women's Policy Studies: Vol. 2). Beverly Hills, Calif.: Sage Publications, Inc., 1977.

Chasen, Barbara. "Toward Eliminating Sex-Role Stereotyping in Early Childhood Classes." *Childcare Quarterly* 6:30-41; Spring 1977.

Chevigny, Bell Gale. *The Margaret Fuller Reader*. Old Westbury, N.Y.: Feminist Press, 1976.

Clark, L. "Fact & Fantasy: A Recent Profile of Women in Academia." *Peabody Journal of Education* 54:103-109, January 1977.

Council on Interracial Books for Children. *Stereotypes, Distortions and Omissions in U.S. History Textbooks*. New York: Racism and Sexism Resource Center for Educators, 1977.

Counseling Psychologist. "Principles for Counseling Specific Subgroups of Women." 1:22-69, 1979.

Crawford, C. "Status of Black Women." *Ebony* 30:26; March 1975.

Curtis, Jean. *Working Mothers*. New York: Doubleday and Co., Inc., 1976.

Dell, Bonnie Thornton."The Dialectics of Black Womanhood."*Signs: Journal of Women in Culture and Society*, Spring 1979. pp. 543-55.

Diamond, Irene. *Sex Roles in the State House.* New Haven, Conn.: Yale University Press, 1977.

Educational Review. "Sex Differences in Examination Performance: Do These Reflect Differences in Ability or Sex-Role Stereotypes?" November 1978. pp. 265-68.

Farmer, Helen, and Backer, Thomas E. *New Career Options for Women: A Counselor's Sourcebook.* New York: Human Sciences Press. 349 pp, 1979.

Frazier, Nancy, and Sadker, Myra. *Sexism in School and Society.* New York: Harper & Row, Publishers, 1973.

Froschl, Merle, and Williamson, Jane. *Feminist Resources for Schools and Colleges: A Guide to Curricular Materials.* Old Westbury, N.Y.: The Feminist Press, 1977.

Garcia, Jesus. "From Blody Savages to Heroic Chiefs." *American Indian Education* 2:15-19; 1978.

Gee, Emma. "Issei: The First Women." *Civil Rights Digest* 6:48-53; Spring 1974.

Gold, S. "Sex Stereotyping in the School." *Education Canada* 17:22-27; Spring 1977.

Grambs, Jean Dresden, ed. *Teaching About Women in the Social Studies—Concepts, Methods, and Materials.* Arlington, Va.: National Council for the Social Studies, 1976.

Grambs, J. D. "Women & Administration: Confrontation or Accommodation?" *Theory into Practice* 15:293-300; October 1976.

Greenberg, Selma. *Right From the Start: A Guide to Non-Sexist Child Rearing.* Boston: Houghton-Miflin, 1978.

"Guidelines for Equal Editorial Treatment of the Sexes; Excerpts from McGraw-Hill Memo." *Today's Education* 64:53; January 1975.

Guttentag, Marcia, and Bray, Helen. *Undoing Sex Stereotypes: Research & Resources for Educators.* New York: McGraw-Hill, 1976.

Hargreaves, D. J. "Sex Roles in Divergent Thinking." *British Journal of Educational Studies* 47:25-32; February 1977.

Harriman, L. C. "Changing Roles: Implications for Home Economics." *Journal of Home Economics* 69:11-13; March 1977.

Hartley, D. "Teacher Definitions of Boys and Girls: Some Consequences." *Resource Education* 20:23-35, November 1978.

Henslee, Tish, and Jones, Peg. "Freedom of Reach for Young Children: Nonsexist Early Childhood Education." Washington, D.C. U.S. Department of Health, Education, and Welfare, Office of Education, 1977.

Hernandez, Aileen. "Small Change for Black Women." *Ms.* August 1974. pp. 16-18.

Hill, H. "Anti-Oriental Agitation and the Rise of Working Class Racism: 1850-1920." *Society* 10:43-48; January 1973.

Horton, P. B. "Sexless Vocabulary for a Sexist Society." *Education Digest* 42:36-38; March 1977.

Howe, Florence. "Sexism, Racism, and the Education of Women." *Today's Education* 62:47-48; May 1973.

Journal of Psychology. "Sex Role Stereotyping and Assertive Behavior. 101:223-28, March 1979.

Journal of Vocational Behavior. "Sex Differences in Perceptions of Familial and Occupational Roles," June 1979. pp. 306-16.

Jung, Betty. "Chinese Immigrants." *Civil Rights Digest* 6:46-47; Spring 1974.

Kahn, Kathy. *Hillbilly Women.* Garden City, N.Y.: Doubleday, 1973.

Katz, Phyllis A. "The Development of Female Identity." *Sex Roles: Journal of Research,* April 1979. pp. 121-33.

Kearns, Martha. *Kathe Kollwitz: Woman and the Artist.* Old Westbury, N.Y.: Feminist Press, 1976.

Kelly, Joan M., and Morgan, Eddye Eubanks. "Combating Classroom Sex Bias." *Journal Home Economics.* Spring 1979.

Kent, Martha. "Competence Is For Everyone." Women's Educational Equity Act Program. Washington, D.C., U.S. Department of Health, Education, and Welfare, Office of Education.

King, Lourdes Miranda. "Puertorriquenas in the United States." *Civil Rights Digest* 6:20-28; Spring 1974.

Lerner, Gerda. *Black Women in White America: A Documentary History.* New York: Random House, 1973.

Lewis, Michael, and Weinraub, Marsha. "Origin of Early Sex-Role Development." *Sex Roles: Journal of Research,* April 1979. pp. 121-33.

Lovier, R. "I am Mind: Mujer Integrate Ahora." *Ms.* February 1975. pp. 3-18.

McDowell, M. B. "New Didacticism: Stories for Free Children." *Language Arts* 54:41-47+; January 1977.

McLure, Gail T. *Women in Science and Technology: Careers for Today and Tomorrow.* Iowa City: The American College Testing Program, 1976.

McCune, Shirley, and Matthews, Martha (eds.) *Implementing Title IX and Attaining Sex Equity: A Workshop Package for Elementary-Secondary Educators.* Prepared for the Title IX Equity Workshops Project of the Council of Chief State School Officers by the Resource Center on Sex Roles in Education, National Foundation for the Improvement of Education. Washington, D.C.: U.S. Department of Health, Education, and Welfare.

McLure, Gail Thomas, and McLure, John W. *Women's Studies.* National Education Association, 1977.

Martin, L. A. "Nonsexist Schools: How Media Specialists Can Help To Make Them." *School Media Quarterly.* 7:128-37; Winter 1979.

Martin, Lois A. "How to Reduce Sex Role Stereotyping." *Today's Education* 67:59-61; November-December 1978.

Mason, Bobbie. *The Girl Sleuth: A Feminist Guide.* Old Westbury, N.Y.: Feminist Press, 1976.

Michael, J. A. "Women/Men in Leadership Roles in Art Education." *Studies in Art Education* 18 No. 2:7-20; 1977.

Mitchell, Joyce Slayton. *I Can Be Anything: Careers & Colleges for Young Women.* Princeton, N.J.: College Board Publication, 1978.

Monteith, M. K. "Alternatives to Burning Sexist Textbooks; ERIC/RCS report. *Reading Teacher* 31:346-50; 1977.

Morgan, Robin. *Going Too Far: The Personal Chronicle of a Feminist.* Westminster, Md.: Random House, Inc., 1977.

Mott, Frank L. (ed.) *Women, Work and Family: Dynamics of Change in American Society.* Lexington, Mass., Lexington Press, 1978.

National Education Association. *Non-Sexist Education for Survival.* Washington, D.C.: the Association.

Nieto, Consuelo. "Chicanas and the Women's Rights Movement: A Perspective." *Civil Rights Digest* 6:36-42; Spring 1974.

Project on Equal Education Rights. *Cracking the Glass Slipper: PEER's Guide to Ending Sex Bias in Your Schools.* Washington, D.C.: Copyright ©1979 NOW Legal Defense Fund.

Public Opinion Quarterly. "Adolescent Perception of Sex Roles in 1968 and 1975." Winter 1977. pp. 459-74.

Rj Associates (Roslyn Kane). *Women in Non-traditional Vocational Education in Secondary Schools.* Washington, D.C.: U.S. Department of Health, Education, and Welfare, Office of Education, February 1978.

Reed, Linda, and O'Donnell, Holly. "Not For Women Only: ERIC/RCS Report." *Language Arts* 2:223-29; 1978.

Reilly, E. M. "Eliminating Sexism: A Challenge to Educators." *Social Education* 43:312-16; April 1979.

Richmond, V. P., and Robertson, D. L. "Women's Liberation in Interpersonal Relations." *Journal of Communication* 27:42-45; Winter 1977.

Rosenfelt, Deborah Silverton. *Strong Women: An Annotated Bibliography for the High School Classroom.* Old Westbury, N.Y.: Feminist Press, 1976.

Russell, Diana E., and Van de Ven, Nicole. *Crimes Against Women.* Millbrae, Calif.: Les Femmes Publishing, 1977.

Sadker, David. *Being A Man—A Unit of Instructional Activities on Male Role Stereotyping.* Washington, D.C.: U.S. Department of Health, Education, and Welfare, Office of Education, 1977.

Sadker, Myra Pollack, and Sadker, David Miller. *Now Upon A Time: A Contemporary View of Children's Literature.* New York: Harper & Row, 1977.

Scher, M. "On Counseling Men." *Personnel & Guidance* 57:252-4; January 1979.

Seifer, Nancy. *Absent from the Majority.* New York: American Jewish Committee, National Project on Ethnic America, 1973.

Sherman, Julia, and Fennema, Elizabeth. "The Study of Mathematics by High School Girls and Boys: Related Variables." *American Educational Research Journal* 2:159-68; 1977.

Silberman, A. "Are the Walls of Sexism Beginning to Tumble?" *Instructor* 86:38; April 1977.

Sipila, H. L. "Women and World Affairs." *Today's Education* 63:66-67; November 1974.

Simpson, Christina J. "Educational Materials and Children's Sex Role Concepts." *Language Arts,* February 1978. pp. 161-67.

Smith, W. S. "Eliminating Sex Role Stereotyping Through Elementary Teacher Education." *Teacher Education* 14:21-7; Autumn 1978.

Smudski, M. D. "Sex and the Single Stereotype." *Educational Horizons* 54:167-71; Summer 1976.

Spock, Benjamin. "How Fathers Can Teach Their Children Sexual Equality." *Redbook* 144:22+; January 1975.

Sprung, B. "Non-sexist Education: A New Focus for Early Childhood Programs." *Children Today,* January 1977. pp. 2-6.

Sprung, Barbara. *Perspectives on Nonsexist Early Education.* New York: Teachers College Press, 1978.

Staples, Robert. *The Black Woman in America.* Chicago: Nelson-Hall Co., 1973. "Stresses and Strains on Black Women." *Ebony* 29:33-36+; June 1974. "The Myth of Black Macho: A Response to Angry Black Feminists." *Black Scholar* 6-7: 21-5; March-April 1979.

Styer, Sandra. "Biographical Models for Young Feminists." *Language Arts* 53:168-74; 1978.

119

Tanner, L. R. "Sex Bias in Children's Response to Literature." *Language Arts* 54:48-50; January 1977.

Tobias, Sheila. *Overcoming Math Anxiety*. New York: W. W. Norton & Co., 278 pp., 1978.

Training Institute for Sex Desegregation. *Strategies for Equality: Volume I, Guidance, Social Studies, Physical Education; Volume II, Vocational Education; Volume III, Multi-Cultural Women's Studies*. New Brunswick, N.J.: Rutgers, The State University of New Jersey, 1979.

Tuchman, Gaye, "Women's Depiction by the Mass Media." *Signs: Journal of Women in Culture and Society*, Spring 1979. pp. 528-42.

U.S. Department of Health, Education, and Welfare. Office of Education. *Focus on Women: A Guide to Programs and Research of the Education Division*. Washington, D.C.: Information Materials Center, 1976.

. . . Conference on the Educational Needs of Black Women, December 16-17, 1975. Washington, D.C.: National Institute of Education, April 1978.

Verheyden-Hilliard, Mary Ellen. *Cracking the Glass Slipper: PEER's Guide to Ending Sex Bias In Your Schools*. Project on Equal Education Rights. Washington, D.C.: Copyright ©1979 NOW Legal Defense Fund.

. . . *A Handbook for Workshops on Sex Equality in Education*. Sex Equity in Guidance Opportunities Project, Washington, D.C.: American Personnel & Guidance Association.

Vidal, Merta. *Chicanas Speak Out: Women, New Voice of La Raza*. New York: Pathfinder Press, Inc., 1971.

Vincenzi, H. "Minimizing Occupational Stereotypes." *The Vocational Guild Quarterly* 25:265-68; March 1977.

Walker, Alice. "In Search of Our Mother's Gardens: The Creativity of Black Women in the South." *Ms.*, May 1974. pp. 64-70.

Weitz, Shirley. *Sex Roles: Biological, Psychological & Social Foundations*. Fairlawn, N.J.: Oxford University Press, 1977.

Wells, M. "National Conference on Non-sexist Early Childhood Education: Report." *Instructor* 86:22-23; April 1977.

Weston, Louise C., and Stein, Sandra L. "A Content Analysis of Publishers Guidelines for the Elimination of Sex-role Stereotyping." *Educational Researcher* 3:13-14; 1978.

Wiles, J. and McNamera, D. "From Bionic Woman to Ultra Man: TV's New Stereotypes." *National Elementary Principal* 56:60-61; January 1977.

Williams, B. "Another Blow to the Black Matriarchy Theory." *Psychology Today*, September 1974. p. 22.

Williams, Maxine, and others. *Black Women's Liberation*. New York: Pathfinder Press, Inc.

Witt, Shirley Hill. "Native Women Today: Sexism and the Indian Woman." *Civil Rights Digest* 6:29-35; Spring 1974.

Women, Money, & Power. Des Plaines, Ill.: Bantam Books, Inc., 1977.

"Women Shou Chung-Kuo-Hua at Parsippani Hills High School." *Senior Scholastic* 103:21; November 1973.

Women's Educational Equity Communications Network. *Resources in Women's Educational Equity, Volume 1; Resources in Women's Educational Equity, Volume II*. San Francisco: Far West Laboratory for Educational Research & Development, 1977, 1978.

Women's Work & Women's Studies, 1973-74. Westbury, N.Y.: Feminist Press, 1977.

Yoshioka, Robert B. "Stereotyping Asian Women." *Civil Rights Digest*, Spring 1974. p. 45.

2632

196